HOUGHTON MIFFLIN COMPANY · BOSTON

New York   Atlanta   Geneva, Ill.   Dallas   Palo Alto

This Is
the
Community
College

EDMUND J. GLEAZER, JR.

Executive Director
American Association of Junior Colleges

FOREWORD

This is an account of one of the fastest-breaking news stories in higher education today. It is the story of the community college. As is obvious from the size and style of the book, I have not intended to write a history or a research document. Others have done that. Rather, this book is meant as an informal introduction to an institution in which growing numbers of citizens are involved and interested.

In my work with the American Association of Junior Colleges, I am often requested to speak to groups interested in knowing more about the two-year community college. Each of the groups I have addressed has expressed its request something like this: tell us about developments in the community college field and give some judgments on what is happening. And that is the reason for this book — to respond briefly with an overview and some conclusions about the nature and potential of the community college in today's society.

The time span is primarily the 1960's. Dramatic expansion of the community college, particularly in the big cities, began in this decade. As I write this, I have before me a list of 200 additional community colleges which will open before the decade ends.

The community college described in this book is not the only kind of junior college. There are also private colleges, some independently supported and others affiliated with church denominations. They, too, have their place and their reason for being, as I can attest from personal experience: for ten years I was president of a private junior college. This book, however, focuses on the species of junior college that has experienced such tremendous change and phenomenal growth during recent years, and is now in the process of determining its future course — the public community college.

I readily confess to a good deal of enthusiasm about the subject of this book. I only hope that I can generate similar excitement and commitment to the community college on the part of others through this presentation. For the community college, to realize its promise and potential, depends heavily on citizen understanding, acceptance and support.

Edmund J. Gleazer, Jr.

Washington, D.C.

CONTENTS

vii

This Is
the
Community
College

1

THE CONTEXT OF
COMMUNITY HIGHER
EDUCATION

Most parents aim to prepare their children to earn a living in today's world. The time when an eighth grade education would suffice is long past. Now a college education is more than ever a necessity. Plan now to start your children toward that college degree by doing your bit to get a Junior College established in Kanabec county.

— Editorial, Ogilvie, Minn., *Sentinel*
February 2, 1967

Increased costs of living have kept many parents from sending their children out of town to colleges and universities. The local college will solve this problem. The personnel needed to operate the institution will aid business and add to our cultural activities. A college town has many advantages. It attracts young people and industry. We believe the Community College will prove a great asset for Mason County and we hope the voters will agree.

— Editorial, Ludington, Mich., *News*
February 16, 1967

We, as a state, are now committed to the proposition that publicly supported education for our young people does not stop with the 12th grade. We are now committed to the proposition that, for all of those who wish it and who have a reasonable degree of aptitude, there shall be college-level education. And the costs, except for tiny token payments, shall be paid from taxes — just as are all the other costs of public education.

— Editorial, Waterbury, Conn., *Republican*
February 26, 1967

F ive hundred new community colleges have sprung up in the last ten years. During a time called "the age of education" by the President of the United States, this was one of the big stories. But it is more than a story of explosive growth, for here was a new kind of college. Higher education was one parent; secondary education the other. But the product of the union claimed recognition in its own right, had an identity of its own — as robust offspring are wont to do.

When the fall semester began in September 1967, seventy community colleges enrolled students for the first time. The year before saw almost that number. Tarrant County Community College opened in Fort Worth, Texas, with more than 4,000 students. But this situation was not unusual. New community colleges in a dozen other states reported initial enrollments in the thousands. In California, Florida, and Mississippi more students began their college work in community colleges than in any other institutions. Several other states had almost reached that point. There was a community college within commuting distance of almost every person in New York State and Florida and California. This would soon be the case in Illinois, Virginia, Michigan, and a score of other states.

Ten years ago, one out of five students in the nation began his work in a community college. Now the number is more than one out of three. Soon it will be one out of two.

Since 1960, community colleges have been established for the first time in twenty major cities. These include Miami with enrollments of more than 20,000, St. Louis with its three

4

campuses, Dallas with its plans for seven campuses. Among the others are Cleveland, Pittsburgh, Philadelphia, Boston, Seattle, and Birmingham.

Within a decade 1,000 publicly supported community colleges will make education beyond the high school available to youth and adults in every state. Just the fact of dramatic growth makes the story newsworthy, but the forces behind the growth are the real story.

Extension of Educational Opportunities

The community college is an adaptation of the educational idea embodied in the junior college. The junior college idea is not a new one but has reached the respectable age of about sixty-five years. Near the beginning of this century William Rainey Harper, president of the University of Chicago, encouraged the school authorities in Joliet, Illinois, to offer two years of classwork beyond the high school. Students who successfully completed this work could be accepted by the University of Chicago in its senior college (third and fourth year of college work). The action signaled the organized beginning of the public junior college. Harper's proposal, however, stemmed from a concern to strengthen the university by assuring a supply of mature and purposive students. He also foresaw institutional benefits if a large number of struggling four-year colleges should consolidate their resources by becoming two-year colleges. As a means for greatly enlarging educational opportunity, the junior college awaited changes in the social and economic life of America.

These changes came rapidly and insistently after World War II. America had expanding international commitments. People moved from rural areas into the cities. The population boomed. Soon there was Sputnik, and America searched its soul and its educational institutions to see what had gone wrong. Why was America not first in the space race? Education became everybody's business. G.I.'s who had gone to college under the first massive federal scholarship program wanted no less for their children.

The nation put its faith in education as a means to many ends: a good job, national security, leadership in the space race, the skilled manpower needed for expanded medical programs. Above all, education was seen as the route to individual achievement, the "open sesame" to economic and social advancement, the way to get ahead.

Since education was considered vital to the well-being of an individual and his family, people began to insist that college doors not be closed to them. This stubborn claim upon education as the means to achievement by increasing thousands led to a condition close to despair in many state capitols. Universities requested higher appropriations in order to expand and to meet mounting costs. Legislators, often under local constituent pressures, introduced measures to establish new colleges in their districts. At the same time other stepped-up programs were demanding more money for better medical care, care of the aged, and improvements in elementary and secondary education. Highways had to be built. Centers of the cities were decaying. Air and water pollution required attention. An air of urgency and crisis prevailed. Decisions were called for. A system of priorities became essential. Policies were needed to guide the use of the financial and personnel resources of the state.

Many of the important issues of postsecondary education moved into the political arena. To what extent should the resources of the state be directed to educational purposes? Who should go to college? What kinds of educational institutions are needed?

Studies were called for. With increasing rapidity as pressures grew, the states inventoried their educational needs and resources and projected future requirements. (California was one of the first.) Recommendations were made. In almost all cases these had several common elements: Opportunity for education beyond the high school should be made available to all. A variety of educational institutions is required; not every institution is to attempt everything. It is necessary to have one or more great centers with libraries, laboratories, research facilities, and a community of highly professional scholars. On the other hand, some educational services ought to be widely diffused throughout the state. Here accessibility is the keynote. Proximity of educational opportunity is a powerful force and calls for widespread facilities and programs.

There was recognition too that some students had demonstrated academic aptitudes and abilities and were well equipped for advanced study. However, the educational program for a state must give opportunity to the large proportion of high school graduates who would benefit from learning experiences more practical than theoretical and who would move into early participation in the occupational and civic life of their communities. The question was, How can an educational system be both highly selective and broadly receptive to a great variety of talent — talent often untested in the academic field or not identifiable by conventional academic measures?

Another important factor was noted: The assumption that formal education terminated on graduation day seemed about as relevant for these times as a horse and buggy was suited to travel on the interstate highways. Some means was required for people to have available throughout their lives educational services appropriate to their interests. Both the great educational centers and the decentralized parts of the system would be affected by this necessity.

These studies, many of them called for by political representatives harassed by severe financial pressures, represent one of the most significant developments in American educational history. For better or worse — and samples of opinion on both sides are volunteered readily — the nature of autonomy of publicly supported colleges and universities was brought under examination in the light of demands for highly diversified educational programs and unprecedented financial requirements for education and other social programs. There was insistence that institutions become much more specific about their purposes and that they yield themselves to a coordinating relationship with other colleges, universities, and a variety of post-secondary institutions.

Out of study, discussion, and heated debate, policies were hammered out for the guidance of legislators, regents, educational administrators, and citizen groups. In these recommendations the community college emerged as an integral part of a total educational program beyond the high school.

State Plans for Community Colleges

Here are some examples of how the community college was viewed in many state plans. In New York State the Board of Regents declared:

> Comprehensive community colleges should be recognized and supported as the basic institutional approach to providing a broader public educational opportunity above the high school level in New York State.

> Two-year and four-year colleges, in a planned, coordinated, and complete system of public higher education, provide essential and complementary, but distinctive services in post-high school education. Therefore, existing two-year colleges should not be converted to four-year baccalaureate college status as an approach to the expansion of college programs in any region in the State.[1]

In Illinois, home of the first publicly supported junior college still in existence (Joliet, 1902), the new master plan for higher education enacted by the legislature in 1966 described the place of the community college. It specified that

> The two-year institutions admit all students qualified to complete any one of their programs, including general education, transfer, technical and terminal, as long as space for effective instruction is available. After entry, the colleges counsel and distribute the students among its programs according to their interests and abilities.

The number and variety of technical and semi-technical programs leading directly to employment be greatly increased primarily through programs established in comprehensive junior colleges.

The junior colleges develop and experiment with programs designed to aid the under-educated student of post-high school age to prepare as speedily as possible for transfer to senior institutions at the junior level or for entry directly into employment from technical and semi-technical programs.[2]

In California, where community colleges have existed for more than half a century, a staff report to the state-level coordinating council emphasized the work of these institutions *within* a broad educational program for the state:

By their history and by their legal mandate California junior colleges are to complement not mimic the other segments of higher education. Such diversity among equals recognizes certain overlapping in the qualifications of students served and the nature of programs offered by the junior colleges, state colleges, and the state university. But the junior colleges are particularly charged with providing services and programs not offered by the other institutions and to educate a more heterogeneous student body.[3]

Questions of Support for the New Institutions

Transmutation of study recommendations into legislative enactments and appropriations was not an easy process. Something had to be done about such unyielding matters as taxes and governmental structures. Although taxpayers in many parts of the country had voted large sums for community college buildings and operating budgets, those subject particularly to the overburdened property tax were more and more often calling for relief. And until recently it was the property tax that represented the major source of revenue for community colleges. Newspapers often editorialized like this:

The turning down of the proposition yesterday [that a community college be sponsored] made it clear that the Commissioners felt that they could not, in good conscience, saddle this extra burden on the people in view of the many other pressing needs which must be met in the future and which, by their very nature, hold priority over others. . . . Taxes are a serious matter in these times. They will become ever more serious in the years just ahead.[4]

Proposals for more aid at the state level raised other questions. A Colorado paper asserted: "When a community college outgrows its own ability to support itself and must accept aid in substantial figures from state government, it loses much of its control."[5] Here was another dilemma. Is it possible to conserve the assumed values of local orientation, control, and responsiveness while authority for funds moves away from the institution's immediate environment?

There was still another deterrent in the form of obsolescent governmental structures. Legislative means had to be sought by which school districts, counties, and county and city governments together could form community college districts. When this rock was turned over, all kinds of rivalries and concerns were exposed: town and country differences, city and county vested interests, and community resistance to identification with a larger and probably different population area — different in race, economic status, and cultural levels.

Attitudes of Existing Colleges and Universities

Retarding community college development in some places was the lack of enthusiastic reception by existing colleges and universities. Questions were raised, naturally, about the effect that greater state financial support of these institutions would have upon appropriations to older members of the educational family. Proposals were heard which called for either elimination of freshman and sophomore work by the senior institutions or marked reduction and consequent diversion of lower-division students to community colleges. In states where appropriations were based only upon the number of students enrolled, anxiety was especially evident. Clearly the cost of educating graduate students and upper-division students was more than that for freshmen and sophomores. Would the legislature understand this and take it into account in formulas for university support?

Further, the universities and other established institutions often questioned the "quality" which might be expected of the new institutions. Could they secure competent staff? Would their "standards" be high enough so that students who transferred to the four-year institutions would do well? How soon could these new colleges meet requirements for regional accreditation? Would it not be better to have the university extend its services than to establish these new institutions?

Higher education's reluctance to accept community colleges was not a problem in all the states. In some, encouragement by the state university in particular was a most important factor.

Building a Sense of Identity

A persisting question which permeated many concerns about the community college was one of definition: What is it? Is it a college or something else? Is it higher education or secondary education? The notion seemed to prevail that if the institution could be filed under either of these categories the answers to all other questions would fall speedily into place. Seldom did the questioners volunteer definitions of higher or secondary education.

Such confusion was bound to exist for a number of reasons. Very often the community college began operations in an existing secondary school. In a state like Maryland and until recently Florida, California and Illinois, district or county school boards had legal responsibility for the colleges along with the public schools. The U.S. Office of Education termed many of the occupational programs in these institutions which did not lead to the bachelor's degree "less than college grade." An officer of one of the nation's foremost foundations replied to a proposal for a grant to community colleges: "Our Board of

Directors has not authorized us to make grants to secondary schools." In California, although the public junior college was identified in legislation as one of the three parts of a system of higher education, the financial and legal underpinnings were still in the secondary system.

Other derivative questions inevitably followed. Do junior college board members identify with the National School Boards Association or with the Association of College and University Governing Boards? Is the place of community college faculty within the American Association of University Professors or with state and national education associations? Some of the reluctance to accept the community college fully stemmed from this uncertainty about how to classify it.

A desire to conform to the stereotype of higher education led to an effort in a number of communities and in the colleges themselves to make the institution a "regular" college — meaning a four-year college. The name "junior" often associated with the community college suggested that the institution was not fully developed, not "grown up." So the community college was viewed as a stage in the evolution of a bachelor's degree-granting institution. Any inclinations in this direction were sure to pose questions. Is this kind of evolution inevitable? Is it desirable? Why create community colleges if they have a built-in tendency to become four-year colleges? What happens to the community college services if the institution goes to a baccalaureate program? Several states adopted a policy, sometimes expressed in legislation, to prevent conversion of a community college into a four-year institution.

There were other contributing factors to encourage aspirations toward senior college status. One of these illustrates the high value placed on social approval. Approximately ten years ago the nation's large philanthropic and corporate foundations initiated substantial activity in the field of higher education. However, community and junior colleges were given little attention. The dramatic action taken by the Ford Foundation in grants to colleges for the improvement of faculty salaries did not extend to a single community college. Recognition by such foundations was a kind of seal of approval. An emerging educational institution strongly desiring public acceptance found its efforts reinforced by only one or two of these new and important opinion shapers.

Another impediment to community college development related to one of its professed major interests: preparation for jobs. Here the new institution encountered a maze of laws, regulations, traditions, and organizations born of a time when vocational education was predominantly at the secondary school level. As more of vocational education necessarily moved beyond the high school, the former ways tended to persist. The community college was viewed, in the sociological sense, as an "invader." This problem was compounded by the society's lack of enthusiasm for vocational education. Seldom was it viewed as a road to economic and social mobility. Theoretically, it was judged beneficial — but for somebody else's children.

Of critical importance in the public's acceptance of the new institutions was the evaluation of their quality. How was this to be determined? How could the quality of a college which would admit almost all students, many of them requiring remedial work for either job preparation or further college experience, be measured? What criteria for excellence would be developed for an institution whose student body was composed of a cross section of the population of the community rather than a slice of the top? High tuition charges, high selectivity, residential programs, liberal arts emphasis — all of the factors commonly associated with prestige of educational institutions — were on one side of the coin, and the publicly supported, open-door, low-cost, commuting student body community college was on the other. On what basis does this kind of institution win its place?

Educational Opportunity and National Policy

In the face of such formidable obstacles, how is it that the community college is rapidly becoming in many states the basic institutional approach to providing a broader educational opportunity above the high school? What has there been in the picture during the last ten years to move it along?

One of the most important forces was this: In a democratic nation which holds that any citizen can become President, or chairman of the board of General Motors, or the pilot of a spacecraft on a voyage to the moon, or can achieve greater status than his father, education is the means. Thus educational opportunity is more than a privilege; it is a citizen's right. And if the great variety of people who exercise this right are to benefit, a broad range of educational experiences is demanded. The population which moves into the nation's colleges will be a cross section of the American people, possessing a wide spectrum of interests, aptitudes, backgrounds, aims, achievements, and cultural determinants. By this reasoning, diversification of educational opportunity is urgently required to match a multitude of individual needs. The community college emerged to meet needs that other institutions could not or would not meet.

Not only did individual aspirations call for broader educational opportunity. There was a national need. In the words of the National Planning Association, ". . . Our nation is confronted with a combination of important and essential goals — some national, some worldwide — which call for more than its human and material resources can support when they are unemployed, under-employed, or under-developed, or are wastefully, carelessly or improperly utilized."[6]

In spite of all of the alarms sounded about the disappearance of jobs, clearly the nation seriously lacked proficient manpower. Society's urgent problems insisted that the human resources of the country not be "under-developed" or "carelessly or improperly utilized." The community college was looked to not only to tap new pools of human talent but to prepare for new kinds of social and vocational responsibilities. A number of national voices called for what was discerned by some to be not just educational improvement but social change. The National Commission on Technology, Automation, and Economic Progress, established by the Congress in 1964, spoke of universal educational opportunity: "The key institutions would be area technical schools and community colleges. . . . The two types of schools might in many instances be merged into community education centers offering both the theoretical foundation of trade, technical and business occupations and the opportunity to 'learn-by-doing' while pursuing liberal education or semi-professional training."[7] The President's Committee on National Goals, the Secretary of Labor, the president of the United States Chamber of Commerce, and the Educational Policies Commission all sounded the same note: The nation should raise its sights to make available at least two years of further education for all high school graduates.

Developing in Congress was an awareness that education was a matter of national policy and that the community college had an important part to play. In a major policy statement the Republican Policy Committee of the United States Senate spoke of "this school-centered society" and pointed out that "in less than ten years we'll have more teachers voting than farmers." "The new electorate," it advised, "will likely opt for whatever method of government will marshal the most resources to keep improving the quality of education."[8]

An increasing number of the legislators were from states and congressional districts in which community college development was taking place. A knowledge of the needs and the potential value of these institutions led to landmark legislative action in 1963. For the first time in federal legislation, in the Higher Education Facilities Act, specific reference was made to public junior colleges and a percentage of grant money was earmarked for them. In other major laws, such as the Allied Health Professions Act of 1966 and the Higher Education Act of 1965, community colleges were included at significant levels.

Further impetus to community college growth through political organization could come as a result of the newly formed Commission of the States. This organization, established through a compact among the states, brings together governors as well as other elected and appointed public officials and educators to consider educational needs and to assemble a body of knowledge about the alternative ways of meeting them. One aim is that well-informed legislative action take place in each of the states. Among the first studies called for was one of the community college.

An Answer to Community Needs

But with all due credit toward recommendations of prestigious national committees and the activities of an educationally minded Congress, the big push that built community colleges was not to be found there. After all, congressmen look toward home for their cues, and national committees are of short duration and limited leverage. Behind the community college growth of the past decade was a grass-roots, organized-at-home coalition for a cause. And the cause? A community college in our town. Here is the way the movement was likely to start:

Dear Sir:

As chairman of the Community Junior College Project for our Shaler Junior High Mothers' Club, a group of two hundred mothers, I have been diligently attempting to acquire all possible knowledge regarding junior colleges, their financing, administering, staffing, etc., etc., and your name has been given me as an authority on this subject.

Our group is well aware how desperately community junior colleges are needed in Pennsylvania, and we have taken that as our one and only project to pursue to what we hope will result in success in obtaining the necessary legislation to make such colleges possible in the near future.

. . . We in Shaler Township and the State of Pennsylvania want and insist upon better educational advantages for our boys and girls. Community junior colleges are desperately needed and wanted, and we intend to obtain same for our students if it is at all within our power, partisan politics or not. We care not one iota whether it be Republican or Democrat who sponsors the necessary legislation — we want better education regardless. Please help and advise us!

In community after community, local groups met the tax problem head-on, promoted changes in state legislation, and often knit together divided segments of the community for the purpose of establishing a college.

The story of the creation of a community college in St. Louis is instructive. The Committee on Higher Educational Needs of Metropolitan St. Louis (a subcommittee appointed by the Governor's Committee on Education Beyond the High School in Missouri) was faced with troublesome questions in 1958. The committee had found in a study that St. Louis was failing to provide local public higher education for its high school graduates. The Committee on Higher Education recommended the establishment of a two-year public college, financed by state and local taxes and by student fees. But there were several major hurdles. The first of these was the necessity of enabling legislation by the state government. The committee drafted proposed legislation and, when the legislature convened in January 1961, the organization of a bi-partisan statewide committee to sponsor junior college legislation was well underway. Officers of the committee represented labor, farmers, industry, business, education, and civic interests throughout the state. Despite a number of hazards, the bill survived in the legislature, because of the widespread interest and support which developed from the committee's efforts. Just before the end of the session, the Missouri legislature passed an excellent junior college law.

The 1961 act allowed for the creation of junior college districts across school district or county lines, provided state level financial support, and gave authority to tax and bond to provide additional financing. The time had come to implement the committee's major recommendation: to create a junior college district in the St. Louis metropolitan area. A committee was formed to spearhead this effort. Local initiative was required by the law as the first step in creating a new district. Volunteers were organized to circulate petitions, and considerably more than the necessary number of signatures were received in both the city and the county. The city's newspapers, and such organizations as the Chamber of Commerce, the Labor Council, League of Women Voters, and parent-teacher associations endorsed the campaign.

The state board approved the proposal and authorized an election to establish the district and to elect the first board of trustees. Thousands of brochures were distributed to inform the citizens of the purpose of the public junior college program, a form of higher education previously unknown in the area.

Opposition to the proposal took several forms. Some citizens favored a county district, which would exclude the city of St. Louis. Others contended that it was "unconstitutional" to set up a public two-year college, and favored state grants to students to permit them to attend institutions of their choice. The committee's major task was encouraging people to vote. The law required a simple majority to establish the district, but the final tally showed a vote of better than two-to-one.

With the assistance of foundation funds, the board began its search for a president and was able to secure the services of a nationally known community college administrator. Three campuses have been established as a result of a successful bond election of $47 million. Classes began in temporary facilities.

This story is told to demonstrate that difficult questions have been answered and formidable obstacles overcome in the establishment of community colleges. The St. Louis story contains many elements that are encountered elsewhere: extension of the use of property taxes for community colleges; the necessity for additional state funds, with the specter of state control as a threat to local decision; jealousies between jurisdictions of government when a community college district is superimposed on county, city or school district lines. These problems were met in a positive way in St. Louis, and the results can be found in successful coordination of city-county resources for the benefit of the citizens of the entire area.

Some reasons for the appeal of the community college idea to PTA groups, chambers of commerce, school board organizations and service clubs are apparent. The community college is close to home. It is of low cost to the student. And usually, as in the case of St. Louis, a local board is elected to govern it, a factor which is of prime importance in many communities.

The past decade was a time of mobility. Young people left the community for their college work and did not return. Interstate highways and developments in air transportation altered the patterns of cities and towns. Business and industry pulled out of some places and expanded activities in others. Centers of population and trade in great metropolitan areas had little basis for identity. The new community college district often transcended political subdivisions which had made sense in a former period. The new district became potentially the basis for a new community — an identifiable area of citizens with some common interests. This was the theme and hope in the editorials of many papers.

A college town has many advantages. It attracts young people and industry. — Michigan

If we do not offer broader education opportunities to the young and old of our area, they will soon seek it elsewhere . . . and our local business, industry, agriculture and commerce will suffer. . . . — Illinois

The proposed Prairie College area is unique in many ways from all other segments of the state. And we believe the area — and its residents — deserve a junior college which reflects this uniqueness. — Illinois

. . . But one of the most important considerations the taxpayer must keep in mind is the eventual growth of the community. The direction of that growth will be determined fundamentally by the facilities which will be in existence. The College will mean a more employable population, a better informed population and a more active and stimulating population. — Montana

The Community College, on Tazewell County soil, has done more to raise the morale locally than anything else since the economic decline in this section and the subsequent "hard times" that have plagued Southwest Virginia. People, in general, can see beyond the horizon of their somewhat dark worlds when they realize their children will have the chance to go to school. — Virginia

The fact that the community or local area was usually required to have a substantial stake in the establishment and support of the new institution meant that questions of community values could not be avoided. What is happening to our community? Is it a desirable place in which to live? Will it survive economically? Will our children want to live here? Are we "keeping up"? The issue of whether to establish a community college — sharpened by the knowledge that there would be additions to the tax bill and that a new kind of district organization would be required — compelled intensive discussion of these questions.

The community college became both the catalyst to stimulate a community consciousness and the product of this consciousness. The college became a symbol of what the community, sometimes almost wistfully, wanted to become. The slow and difficult process of establishing new alignments and groupings of people into concentrations of somewhat common interests was unexpectedly facilitated by the development of the college. In building the college the groundwork was laid for identification of new aggregations of people with potentially important values of membership and social participation.

It was out of this ground, then, that a new kind of educational institution arose in America. Eclectic and opportunistic, the community college had its force and meaning rooted in the urgent needs of community life, in the process of change and in the faith that among the ways to better life none was more important than education.

Some will charge that such a faith is naïve and unrealistic. But whether it is warranted is not the question. That it motivated a tremendously significant change in the educational program of this nation in the 1960's is a social fact. Emergence of the community college was a logical and necessary part of that change.

NOTES

[1] "The Comprehensive Community College: A Policy Statement of the New York State Board of Regents," Albany, February 27, 1967.

[2] *A Master Plan — Phase II for Higher Education in Illinois.* Springfield: State of Illinois, Board of Higher Education, December 1966.

[3] "A Consideration of Issues Affecting California Public Junior Colleges," staff report for presentation to the Coordinating Council for Higher Education, January 25–26, 1965, Sacramento, April 1965.

[4] "Commissioners' Decision Result of Careful Study," Westchester, Pa., *Local News,* December 23, 1966.

[5] "Community Controls," Grand Junction, Colo., *Sentinel,* December 26, 1966.

[6] "Unlimited Demands and Limited Resources: How Can America Meet the Challenge," National Planning Association Joint Statement, *Looking Ahead,* Supplement 7. Washington: The Association, 1962.

[7] National Commission on Technology, Automation, and Economic Progress, *Technology and the American Economy.* Washington: U.S. Government Printing Office, 1966.

[8] Republican Policy Committee, United States Senate, *Where the Votes Are.* Washington: U.S. Government Printing Office, 1966.

2

THE COMMUNITY
COLLEGE MOVEMENT:
AN OVERVIEW

A concurrent resolution recognizing the contributions made by the Florida Community Junior College Program upon the final implementation of the state-wide master plan established by the 1957 Legislature.

. . . Whereas, Florida will be the "first state in the nation" to complete a state plan making community junior colleges available to all the people of the State, and

Whereas, since their establishment Florida community junior colleges have rendered educational services to over 500,000 persons, and

Whereas, these community junior colleges in partnership with the state university system have provided Florida citizens a program of higher education which is among the most comprehensive in the nation with respect to the needs of business, industry, and the communities of the state. . . . NOW, THEREFORE, Be It Resolved by the House of Representatives of the State of Florida, the Senate Concurring:

That the Legislature expresses its pride in the development of this program of post high school education and hereby recognizes the national leadership of the state in the planned and orderly development of a state-wide junior college system and the contributions this program of higher education is making to the people of Florida. . . .

— Florida 1967 Legislature. Resolution
SCR 1537, HCR 2876
Tallahassee: Florida Senate, June 9, 1967

Wh-hen Florida's newest community college opens in 1969, the state will have made educational history by completing a plan, made in 1957, to put community college services within commuting distance of 99 per cent of its citizens. On June 20, 1967, the state legislature, meeting at Tallahassee, took note of this remarkable achievement. Florida was first to make these educational services available throughout an entire state. Twenty-eight community colleges are strategically located from Miami to Jacksonville to Pensacola.

This systematic and orderly expression of an educational plan deserves recognition on several counts. Careful studies led to a "master plan." Priorities were established for the founding of new institutions. The plan involved universities as well as community colleges. Provision was made for coordination among the various parts of the state's program in post-high school education. Another good reason for a close look at Florida's plan and progress is the fact that most of the other states either are experiencing similar development or will do so within the next few years.

One out of five persons beginning college in Florida in 1957 went to the community junior college (as it is called there). In 1967, ten years later, the number was two out of three (see accompanying chart). Enrollments soared during this period in all the institutions of higher education but the pattern of distribution of students among the various colleges and universities changed markedly. Along with its emphasis upon community colleges, Florida took the lead in another somewhat novel concept. Actually, the idea was not new, but its expression in public education was. Two universities were founded,

24

Florida Public Junior Colleges

Distribution of All First-Time-in-College On-Campus Students Among Florida Institutions of Higher Learning Fall 1957 to Fall 1966

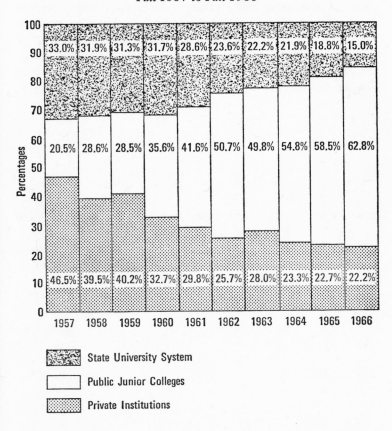

Source: *Board of Regents, State of Florida (Tallahassee, Florida), 1966.*

Florida Atlantic and West Florida, to concentrate on the third and fourth year of the bachelor's degree program and the first graduate degree. No freshman and sophomore courses were offered. Community college graduates were to be a leading source of students for these new universities.

California is mentioned early in any discussion of public junior colleges. The first such institution in that state opened more than fifty years ago. Now there are eighty junior colleges, enrolling more than half a million full- and part-time students. Seventy-five per cent of all full-time lower-division students (first two years) attending a public college in California are in a community college. By order of the state legislature, more-over, all high school districts were to be in a junior college district by the end of 1967. More than 90 per cent of the state's population is now within commuting distance of a community college.

The Spread of Community Colleges

Other states are moving in the direction taken by Florida and California. Only a handful of the 102 counties in Illinois are not covered by either an existing or a proposed community college district. As a consequence of the big step taken by the state in its 1965 legislation, twenty-five community colleges either have opened or are preparing to open. Appropriations for buildings and equipment by the legislature in 1967, although less than requested, reached the impressive level of $125 million.

In New York State 85 per cent of the people are within commuting distance of a public two-year college. Several now being organized will bring New York close to California and Florida in extent of accessibility.

Recognition of the need to expand and broaden opportunities in New Jersey has led to a county college system. The four county colleges (community colleges) opened in September 1966, were the first. Two more began in 1967. Six others have been established and will soon enroll students. Of the state's twenty-one counties, only three have taken no official action toward creation of these institutions.

Michigan has twenty-four community colleges (serving 60,000 students) which are within reach of most of the residents of that state. Ten more are on the verge of being established.

Pennsylvania looks toward a statewide coverage with thirty institutions. The first opened in Harrisburg in 1964. Characteristically, it got its start in temporary facilities but in 1967 dedicated a new campus and received full accreditation by the Middle State Association of Colleges and Universities. The Community College of Philadelphia began operations in the center of that city in 1965. Pittsburgh followed in 1966. Fourteen other community colleges have opened since or are preparing to open.

These seven states contain 40 per cent of the population of this country. In each of them, policy has been adopted which will make community college services available to almost all residents. This substantial sample represents developments in most of the nation. There are community colleges in Hawaii and Puerto Rico, the Virgin Islands and Alaska. Only Maine and South Dakota have no public two-year institutions. California leads the list with eighty. New York and Texas approach forty. Illinois, Florida, and Michigan are in the next bracket with about thirty.

In October 1967, more than nine hundred junior and community colleges enrolled 1,700,000 students. Six hundred fifty of the two-year colleges are publicly supported community colleges. Their enrollments totaled 1,550,000. Two hundred seventy-five were church-related and independent junior colleges with enrollments of 150,000.

The Trend Toward a Comprehensive Institution

Questions are often asked about the differences between a community college and a junior college. "Junior college," the older term, describes an institution which offers the first two years of college. Preparation of students who transfer to the four-year college or university is usually one of its major functions. There is general recognition now that the community college is a kind of junior college but with broader educational functions and most often supported by public funds.[1] A few community colleges are privately supported. The term "community college" was used by the President's Commission on Higher Education in 1947 to refer to public junior colleges which were "community centered" and "community serving." Both junior colleges and community colleges sometimes are referred to as two-year colleges.

For the most part, the community college has become a comprehensive institution with a great variety of programs to match the cross section of the community represented in its students. The concept of comprehensiveness, although still a subject for occasional debate, generally is accepted. This means preparation for employment as well as transfer to four-year colleges and includes a number of other community-related services. The comprehensive community college exists to give students opportunity beyond the high school to find suitable lines of educational development in a social environment of wide range of interests, capacities, aptitudes, and types of intelligence.

In several states there has been a trend toward the comprehensive community college and away from specialized vocational and technical schools at the postsecondary level. One of many groups which have noted and encouraged this change is the Governor's Commission on Education Beyond the High School in North Carolina.

> We believe that the industrial education centers and the community colleges will tend to become more alike than unlike; that the perpetuation of two increasingly similar but separate systems of post-high school institutions of two-year grade cannot be justified either on educational or on economic grounds; and that state-level supervision of the two systems by different agencies will lead to undesirable competition, lack of effectiveness and efficiency, and economic waste. We recommend that the State develop one system of public two-year post-high school institutions offering college parallel, technical-vocational-terminal, and

adult education instruction tailored to area needs; and that the comprehensive community colleges be subject to state-level supervision by one agency.[2]

Not only in North Carolina, but in New York, Virginia, and other states, vocational schools beyond the secondary level have become comprehensive community colleges. In some states the broadening has taken another direction: responsibility has been added for those students whose eyes are not on the bachelor's degree. All of this means that most community colleges today aim toward a comprehensiveness which is finally determined by the educational needs of the community, the resources available, the philosophy of those responsible for the college program, and the choices of the students. Continuing education, counseling services, and remedial programs further extend the span of the institution.

Organizational Structure

Evolution of the work of these new institutions has been accompanied by important changes in organizational structure and financing patterns. Today's community colleges have financial and population bases much broader than those of their predecessors. The large districts created include many high school districts or even bigger areas such as one or more counties. The organizational base may be a metropolitan area or a city and county. The service area of the college commonly is becoming the legal district. When costs are spread over larger tax districts and borne by larger populations, the depth and variety of services required are more feasible economically.

Convenient access by commuting students in the expanded districts often requires several campuses or colleges. For example, the Junior College District of St. Louis-St. Louis County organized three campuses in population centers. Dallas County Junior College in its second year of operation acquired land for six campuses throughout the county. There are eight community colleges in Los Angeles under one district administration. Miami-Dade Junior College has two campuses and plans for at least one more. These illustrate the common pattern of organization: a large district with multiple units under centralized administration. Effort is made to locate the campuses so that travel time for the student is no more than one hour.

A board of trustees is elected or appointed with legal responsibility for the district. The board appoints a president as chief executive officer. A significant development of recent years had been the move toward giving boards jurisdiction over community colleges only, rather than making them responsible for the entire local public school program from kindergarten through the community college. Only a handful of the combined school-college boards now exist.

The concept of a local board whose sole responsibility is the operation and management of the college has been influenced by the very size of the operations in many cities. The community college enrolls thousands of students. It employs large numbers of faculty. The budgetary implications are great enough to justify the full attention of the board of control for this institution alone. Another reason frequently given is that post-secondary education is sufficiently different from elementary and secondary education to require a different set of viewpoints toward the institution's job.

Separate organization at the local level has its counterpart at the state level. Thirty-eight states have agencies with varying degrees of responsibility for community colleges. In California, recent legislation has substituted a state junior college board for the former Bureau of Junior Colleges in the state department of education. Florida has a division of community junior colleges in the state department of education. On the other hand, the Massachusetts Board of Regional Community Colleges is appointed by the governor and is not part of the department of education. This is also the case in Minnesota. New legislation in Illinois set up a state junior college board to take over functions previously carried out by the office of the state superintendent of public instruction. That board in turn is represented on a board for higher education which is the state's coordinating agency for higher education.

Although there are many variations in state-level organization, a common element is evident. Community college activity has reached a significance which requires a state agency with distinct accountability for this institution as well as the duty of representing it in coordinate relationships with other educational interests of the state.

State Financial Support

For a number of reasons state-level responsibilities have increased. If chaos is to be avoided, some authoritative body is needed to establish conditions under which a community college district can be formed. This agency investigates potential enrollments of the proposed college, population of the district, assessed valuation, and evidence of need and local interest. The interest in most cases must be demonstrated by some financial support. Minimum standards are prescribed to insure quality of instruction, breadth of educational opportunity, and effectiveness of operation. The agency usually certifies that the college is meeting these requirements as the basis for receipt of state funds.

A word about other standards. The college will move along as rapidly as possible to exceed minimum requirements and to qualify for full recognition by the accrediting agency for the region in which it is located. This process requires usually not less than three or four years after the institution opens. The six regional accrediting agencies have procedures now which acknowledge problems faced by new institutions, particularly in establishing eligibility for federal support programs. A letter can be issued to the effect that the institution is a candidate for accreditation. Such certification is usually sufficient for participation under most federal acts.

An obvious reason for more state interest in community colleges is the increasing financial load which the state is carrying. Formerly local public junior colleges were supported largely by local school districts and some income from nominal tuition charges. In some states — California and Illinois among them

— there was no tuition. With inclusion of community colleges in state plans for post-high school education a question was heard more and more frequently: Why does the state appropriate a great deal of money for its public colleges and universities while directing little to the public junior colleges, which have an increasing proportion of college students? Another factor was persuasive for state support. As long as the community college district relied principally upon its own financial resources, those parts of the state which had the wealth also had the colleges. Other areas, with a critical need for such services, did not get them because their financial capacity would not permit it. A major deterrent to community college development and a barrier to equalization of educational opportunity was removed as the states increased their share of financial support, for both operations and buildings.

Although the states have a variety of practices in financing community colleges, there are some similarities. In descending order, revenue is from the state, the district, and the student. In a paper submitted to the Education Commission of the States, Dr. S. V. Martorana reported that a median of 20 per cent of operating costs was borne by the student in twenty-nine reporting states. In the same states a median of 31.5 per cent of operating costs was met by the locality and of 54 per cent by the state.[3] What do these figures mean in terms of charges to the student? California has no tuition for in-district students. In Florida tuition is not more than $200 for the year, and in Illinois it is about the same since the 1965 enactment. In New York State it ranges from $300 to $400 except in the community colleges under the City University of New York where nothing is charged. The California and New York figures are approximately the low and high. Strong community sentiment exists to hold cost to the student as low as possible.

Federal Financial Support

Not much money has been available from federal government sources for program support; however, the amount is increasing. The Higher Education Act of 1965 authorized funds for library materials. As much as 22 per cent of appropriations was set aside for public and private two-year colleges under the Developing Colleges Program. In 1966, fifty-two junior and community colleges participated in the Community Services Program of the same act.

Upward Bound, the antipoverty program, makes funds available to two-year colleges, as well as the four-year institutions, to establish special summer programs for high school students who are considered to have college potential but who, for economic or cultural reasons, might not continue their education. The Allied Health Professions Act of 1966 authorized the payment of $500 per student to colleges (including community colleges) for the operating costs of health technology programs, besides funds for planning and carrying out advanced traineeships. Other federal measures in which community colleges have had a part are the Adult Basic Education Program and the Manpower Development and Training Program.

Vocational education money has been channeled to many community colleges since the passing of the Vocational Education Act of 1963. Major new legislation to expand support is pending in the House of Representatives. Nevertheless, in the opinion of community college representatives, the amounts directed to their institutions do not take into account the greatly increased number of post-high school vocational programs they now offer. In testimony before a House subcommittee on education, on April 13, 1967, a spokesman for the American Association of Junior Colleges asserted that many young people and adults in several states benefit minimally if at all from the federal Vocational Education Act because vocational education boards in those states give little or no support to community colleges and other college-level vocational education programs.

One of the older federal acts which has been of much assistance is the Higher Education Facilities Act of 1963, which authorized 22 per cent of available facilities funds for public junior colleges. State or local matching funds are required. The Higher Education Amendments Act of 1966 increased benefits to 23 per cent in fiscal 1968 and 24 per cent in fiscal 1969. Total funds allotted to public junior colleges were approximately $491 million for the three fiscal years 1967–1969. However, there has been a wide gulf between authorizations and appropriations. Each year the appropriation for college facilities has been substantially less than the authorization. For fiscal 1968, $100 million was appropriated for public junior colleges.

State-level financial assistance for community college construction is increasing markedly. Illinois illustrates the trend. Until adoption of the junior college bill signed by Governor Otto Kerner July 15, 1965, there was no state money for buildings and site acquisition. The new act authorized state funds for site, site improvements, and construction in separate districts in the amount of three-fourths of approved project costs up to 1971 and 50 per cent of these costs after that date. The larger proportion in the earlier years was to stimulate broader organization of community college districts.

Money Problems

The necessity, which still exists in many places, to finance buildings and equipment out of local property tax revenues has often slowed the establishment of needed services. A result has been the move toward more state and federal assistance. However, numerous districts have received significant local funding. Dallas County began operations for its college with a successful bond election in the amount of $41.5 million. St. Louis voted $47 million, as did Peralta Junior College District (Oakland, California). There are other success stories but also many areas in which bond elections failed repeatedly.

Very probably the trend toward greater state and federal assistance will continue. In a few states — Florida and Minnesota, for example — all of the money for buildings comes from the state. More often there is a shared arrangement in which the junior college district, the state, and increasingly the federal government all participate.

"Where is the money going to come from?" That is a question often heard, and its importance cannot be minimized.

Community college operations and plant requirements are not insignificant in size. At one time "small college" and "junior college" were terms used almost interchangeably. Not any longer. In its seventh year of operation Miami-Dade Junior College reported in 1967 more than 20,000 students. Cuyahoga County Community College in Cleveland had an enrollment of more than 10,000 in its fourth year. Many California junior colleges have more than 10,000 students. In 1966, sixty-five community colleges each enrolled more than 5,000 students. What does this mean in terms of facilities costs?

Rules of thumb must be used with caution. However, a fair estimate of the price of a 5,000-student campus is about $20 million. Acquisition of site is additional. Some planners recommend 100 to 150 acres minimum. Most colleges are procuring more — 200 to 400 acres. Some boards have recognized that land is a good investment and that it will not get cheaper. These figures obviously do not apply to downtown, inner-city construction.

The Community College's First Steps

Although community colleges today usually have their own facilities, they often begin in existing structures that have been modified to permit enrollment of students as soon as possible. Dallas and Philadelphia started out in remodeled downtown department stores. Several institutions had their beginnings in former hospitals or military installations. Some get under way in the wing of a large high school plant. Rock Valley College in Illinois adapted the facilities of a dairy farm to meet its initial needs. A few colleges have experimented with "instant campuses": prefabricated buildings which can be assembled quickly and then moved to another site for another college when permanent structures are completed. In a few cases an entire new campus is developed before any classes begin. Tarrant County Community College in Fort Worth went into operation this way, as did the College of the Desert in California. But regardless of how they first open, most community colleges now have their own identifiable facilities. People driving by can say: "There is the community college." While this might appear to be a minuscule observation, it represents a conspicuous change in conditions from those of a short generation ago, when public junior colleges were more often than not guests of uncertain tenure in surplus space provided by the local high school.

Profile of the Community College

An overview of community college activity throughout this nation shows the states using a variety of ways to organize and finance community college services. Although no national consensus is apparent, there is enough agreement to suggest a general profile of this developing institution, with the caution repeated that some state and local divergencies exist. A national overview would see the community college as:

1. A part of higher education in a state plan.
2. Receiving an increasing proportion of financial support from the state.
3. Established and operated under standards set at the state level.
4. Admitting all students who can benefit by a program.
5. Charging little or no tuition.
6. Having almost entirely students who commute.
7. Increasing the number and variety of technical and semi-professional programs.
8. Comprehensive in its programs.
9. Providing services to aid undereducated students of post-high school age.
10. Looking to a state-level junior college board for coordination of planning, programs, and services and for state aid.
11. Represented in a state board or council for coordination with other institutions of higher education.

12. Having a separate and distinct district board, facilities, and budget.
13. Locally initiated and controlled, with sufficient state participation to maintain standards.

The Role of Universities, Foundations, and National Organizations

A panoramic view of community colleges in the United States in 1968 would not be complete without mention of three other influential and interfusing components of the whole enterprise: universities with service and research interests; national foundations; and national organizations in business, the professions, and industry.

More than a dozen leading universities and that many more state colleges give a great deal of attention to the community college. They prepare faculty and administrators and extend their facilities and assistance to those people who want to keep up professionally through conferences, institutes, or personal consultation. Typical examples of their helpfulness are sessions for new presidents, board members, and financial officers. A number of these programs began under grants from the W. K. Kellogg Foundation in 1960. After several years of foundation subsidy, the universities assumed a major share of financial responsibility to keep the services going. It would be difficult to overstate the importance of these university contributions to the community college. Useful channels of communication now exist between university personnel and community college administrators and faculty where some years ago there was often lack of understanding and even distrust.

Both the doctorate and the master's degree programs to prepare community college staff generally involve internships. This situation has further encouraged interaction between the university and the community college, with marked benefits for both. The groundwork has been established for the massive increase in effort now required to meet imperative needs for research and for personnel development.

Without question the national philanthropic and corporate foundations are among the shapers of American education. Their "venture capital" has enabled public institutions to have resources above public funds with which to experiment and to develop better ways of doing things. Beyond this, the fact that a well-known foundation makes grants to an educational institution seems to say to the public, "Here is something worth watching; it shows promise; it is worth betting on."

A number of foundations are interested in the community college and its potential. Over a period of several years the W. K. Kellogg Foundation has made grants totaling several million dollars. It assisted in the rapid growth of the associate degree program in nursing as well as other semiprofessional and technical programs. Junior college leadership centers for preparation of administrators were financed initially by the foundation, and its support continues. Money has gone also to the American Association of Junior Colleges to expand and strengthen its services.

The Carnegie Corporation of New York has helped in the appraisal and development of student personnel work in junior colleges as well as in the examination of more effective ways to prepare faculty. Better training of faculty also has been an interest of the Ford Foundation. The Esso Educational Foundation supports some new approaches to faculty education, and its funds made possible important moves to facilitate transfer of students from two-year to four-year colleges.

Grants from the United States Steel Foundation have assisted in a searching look at the community college teacher and his professional interests and needs. Technical education and planning in the community college field have been the objects of grants from the Alfred P. Sloan Foundation. The Sears-Roebuck Foundation has been interested in more effective interpretation of the services of community and junior colleges. Money has been appropriated to encourage and aid in the establishment of curriculums to prepare students for public service occupations.

The fact that no less than $4 billion worth of construction will be planned and contracted for by these institutions within the next ten years has been noted by the Educational Facilities Laboratories of New York. Funds have been allotted to junior and community colleges and to the American Association of Junior Colleges toward more effective planning.

Not all of the foundations that have made grants in the community college field have been named. Those mentioned represent many with an increasing sensitivity to the promise of this new institution to help solve urgent and troublesome problems in an urban society.

One of the most influential forces in community college development today is the vast but functional network joining the community college and national organizations in health, business, industry, education, and other areas. This is a phenomenon of very recent origin. An early example of the effectiveness of such relationships was the pilot effort of the National League for Nursing, the American Association of Junior Colleges, the Columbia University School of Nursing, and several community colleges to determine the worth of an associate degree program to prepare bedside nurses. This pattern is common now in many other fields. In response to social and economic changes following World War II, rapidly developing scientific and medical advancements, and concerns about the suitability of education for nursing, important studies of nursing practice were instituted by national nursing organizations and the universities. In one such study, conducted by the Division of Nursing Education, Teachers College, Columbia University, a multidisciplinary group developed a concept that the function of nursing, in the broad occupational sense, could be thought of as *spectrum-ranged:*

> "The range of activities involved in performing nursing functions was seen to extend along a continuum from the simplest to the most complex; requiring deftness ranging from simple dexterity to a high degree of skill and expertness; involving responsibilities ranging from following repetitive uncomplicated routines

to making critical judgments and independent decisions about the appropriate nursing action. Nursing activities ranged from those requiring little or no special knowledge to a great deal of technical and professional skill attainable only through an extensive period of systematic training through higher education."[4]

If the spectrum theory is accepted, there can be an assignment of appropriate functions to personnel trained to that level or kind of activity. Soon after the publication of the *Program for the Nursing Profession,* which grew out of a study of the role of registered nurses, Mildred Montag proposed a new type of worker, the nursing technician, "to help meet nursing needs, and a new type of technical education program in nursing to prepare the technician in two years' time in junior and community colleges."[5]

A five-year Cooperative Research Project in Junior and Community College Education was launched to determine whether a nursing program could become an integral part of a junior or community college and whether a program of technical education in nursing to prepare its graduates for state licensure could be effective. Although evaluation must continue, the existence of more than three hundred such programs in the country now attests to their valuable place in meeting the nation's demand for more well trained workers in the health fields. This project was important not only in its effect upon patterns of preparing nurses but also as conspicuous recognition by an important professional organization of the potential value of community colleges in meeting urgent manpower needs. This was to be the first of many partnership efforts involving professional associations, foundations, colleges, universities, community colleges, and other private and public agencies.

Another recent illustration is in the process by which *A Guide for Health Technology Program Planning* was formulated. The colleges collaborated with the National Health Council, which includes some seventy health agencies, among them the American Medical Association, the American Hospital Association, and the National League for Nursing.

Joint efforts have been undertaken with the American Dental

Association, the National Council for Medical Technology Education, the International Association of Chiefs of Police, and the American Society of Planning Officials. Furthering the work of community colleges in preparation of people for retail store management and sales is the liaison with the Institute of Distribution, which includes the largest retail chain stores in the country as members. Working relationships are in effect also with the National Restaurant Association, the National Hotel and Motel Association, and similar groups in a variety of fields.

Nationally, too, the community colleges are linked in projects of mutual interest to the American Library Association, the American Educational Publishers Institute, the Educational Testing Service, the College Entrance Examination Board, and other such agencies.

There exists in this country a complex system of associations and organizations which represent a variety of occupational and interest groups. An element in the present community college picture which is vastly different from that of even a decade ago is the awareness which these organizations and the community college have of each other. Cooperative activities have been brought about and communication has been improved, resulting in more effective educational programming, and thus in greater benefits to those who enroll in community colleges. It is not an overstatement to say that the community college has a new sense of being needed and wanted as it takes its place in the mainstream of American life. In short, a base for constructive and productive relationships has been established through this kind of cooperation.

NOTES

[1] "COMMUNITY COLLEGE. A two-year institution of higher education, generally public, offering instruction adapted in content, level, and schedule to the needs of the community in which it is located. Offerings usually include a transfer curriculum (credits

transferable toward a bachelor's degree), occupational (or terminal) curriculums, general education, and adult education." — *Handbook of Data and Definitions in Higher Education,* A Service of the Joint Committee on Data and Definitions in Higher Education Sponsored by the American Association of Collegiate Registrars and Admissions Officers, 1962.

[2] "Education Beyond the High School," report of the Governor's Commission on Education Beyond the High School, Raleigh, N.C., 1962.

[3] S. V. Martorana, "Community-Centered, Post–High–School Education," paper prepared for the Education Commission of the States, April 26, 1967.

[4] Bernice E. Anderson, *Nursing Education in Community Junior Colleges.* Philadelphia: J. B. Lippincott Company, 1966, pp. 5–6.

[5] *Ibid.*

3

DEFINING THE
COMMUNITY
COLLEGE'S ASSIGNMENT

One of the long-time basic education needs in this state has been the system of colleges located in communities throughout the state to serve those who cannot and who should not, because of various reasons, attempt to gain immediate admittance to the four year schools. The community college, bringing education to the doorstep of thousands of North Carolinians who might not have otherwise attempted college, is filling the need for which it was designed.

— Editorial, Raleigh, N. C., *Times*
February 2, 1967

How good is the community college? That question, to be answered, needs a sharper point. You might as well ask: How good is the automobile or the boat? Judgment, obviously, has to be made in terms of the requirements of the user. If a man and his wife want to explore leisurely and comfortably the inlets and creeks off Chesapeake Bay, a deep-draft, ocean racing sailboat is not good for them. The suburban housewife, with her den of cub scouts to chauffeur around on a Saturday morning, will not be enthusiastic about the merits of a two-seater, four-on-the-floor, 140-miles-per-hour sports car. "Goodness" — or the utility of something — can be judged only in terms of the job the thing is supposed to do. If it does that job well, it is good. It may be a very inexpensive, plain, and simple tool — like a corkscrew. If it has utility, it is of high value. If it does not work, however great the cost, however fancy the finish, however handy the thing for other purposes, in terms of this job it is no good.

So the question, to make sense, has to be rephrased: How good is the community college for the job it is designed to do? And that leads to the heart of the matter: What is the job?

"All Available Talent"

The major assignment of the community college is to *extend* educational opportunity. It does this as an important part of society's need to *broaden* educational opportunity. In the Foreword to *Access to Higher Education,* by Frank Bowles, this necessity was viewed as an international concern:

The present expansion in education is not only vastly increasing the number of students; it is also drawing them from many more diverse social origins. This trend should be encouraged further. We should cast our net wider and wider in order to identify, to catch and to bring within the scope of education all available talent, wherever it may be found.[1]

Richard Pearson, president of the College Entrance Examination Board, has seen in this societal need the implications for educational services:

The elementary and secondary schools of the country are now fully committed to the entire cross-section of American youth, whatever the differences are that exist among them. The persistent annual increase in college enrollments can only be interpreted as meaning that the colleges and universities of the country are being asked to assume an equally broad responsibility for all the youth of the country, at least through the fourteenth year. From the perspective of the individual young people who will join the student population of the future, the curriculum of the country's colleges and schools must somehow accommodate all of them in all their individuality.[2]

That the call for greater breadth of educational opportunity was made by a spokesman for an organization occasionally regarded as restrictive in its concept of talent is itself impressive. Mr. Pearson might have added to the complexity of the educational task if he had referred to the dramatic increase in adults seeking educational opportunity as well as to "the youth of the country."

The well-known sociologist Robert Havighurst, formerly of the University of Chicago, sees the community college playing a key role:

The commitment of the American society to the maintenance and expansion of opportunity for post-secondary education will be realized primarily through the junior colleges, which may have to double their total enrollment during the next five years. The junior college must meet a variety of needs that other higher institutions cannot or will not meet. It must do this at relatively low cost.[3]

These statements seem to derive from a common conviction: that all available talent should be nurtured by as much education as is necessary to bring it to flower. The commitment made by elementary and secondary schools to the entire cross section of American youth is to be required now of the nation's colleges and universities, at least through the fourteenth year. Taking its place in the educational scheme, the junior college is to meet innumerable needs that other higher institutions cannot or will not meet. Now, how does it accomplish this task?

Accessibility

In the words of the Raleigh *Times,* it brings the college opportunity to the "doorstep" of the student. Ask almost anyone attending a community college why he is there and he will be likely to say: "Because it's close to home." This is considered an unsatisfactory reason by all kinds of people. Some psychologists say the student would be much better off if he cut the dependency ties with his home and went away to college. Some protagonists for the community college would hope that a more prestigious reason could be given, such as "I thought the teaching would be superior." But although this straightforward, utilitarian answer makes few educators happy, it is true. A great number of students are there because the college is close by. Proximity is a factor in college attendance.

Seven per cent of the high school graduates in a Florida county were entering college the year before the community college was established. Ten years later, 52 per cent of the graduates began college, 45 per cent of them in the community college. The fact that the college was there made the difference. Another example of proximity and attendance patterns is available in Chicago. Chicago City College operates in eight localities thoughout the city. Continuing studies show that the percentage of the college-age group enrolled at the campuses decreases markedly with distance.

There are numerous factors to account for the large proportion of students who cannot or will not go away to college. Many adults have family responsibilities and jobs in the area. Other students cannot afford the added expense of board and room. Some are just not ready to leave home. Regardless of the reasons, and whether or not these are judged important by the critic, it is evident that a community college within commuting distance attracts large numbers of people who would not be in college under other circumstances.

Locating the community college close to the homes of its students is firm policy in most states. As already mentioned, California, Florida, New York, Michigan, Pennsylvania, Illinois, and New Jersey, with 40 per cent of the nation's population, have acted to make community colleges easily accessible to their residents. They are followed closely by other states in which the policy directions are similar.

Cost to Student

What is the reason given most often for not going to college? "I couldn't afford it." One of the major tasks of the community college is to reach those who could not pay the cost of going to other institutions. The student minimizes his expenses by living at home. Tuition fees are low or nonexistent.

A look at the students' financial backgrounds support the testimony, "If it were not for the community college with its low cost, I would not be in college." A large percentage are the first generation of college-goers in the family. Over half of the students hold part-time jobs. In a city in Florida where there are both a community college and a publicly supported state university, twice as many students reporting family incomes above $10,000 were enrolled in the university.

Although a good deal of variation exists among the cities and states, a number of careful studies show that often the socioeconomic background of the community college student is different from that of his counterpart in another college or a university. Relatively far fewer families represented are in the professional and managerial groups. Many more are in blue-collar occupations and live in low-status neighborhoods.

One of the most serious barriers to college attendance has been lowered impressively by the community college: the cost to the student. The range, as reported previously, is from no tuition charge in California to perhaps $400 per year in New York State. About $200 would be a safe estimate as a national average. Community opinion throughout the country has strongly supported minimal tuition fees. However, the pressures from rising costs and the multiplying of public services will require a determined effort to keep the community college financially accessible. If the effectiveness of this new institution as an instrument for social and economic mobility is not to be blunted or destroyed, financial barriers must not exist.

Admission Policy

The community college offers a broad array of services. Under an "open-door" admissions policy, various educational programs are available to people of different aptitudes, interests, achievements, and ages. Professional counseling assists the student in selecting the lines of educational development most suitable for him.

Although publicly supported community colleges are predominantly open-door institutions, admission to programs *within* the college is on a selective basis. In California, all high school graduates may enter the junior colleges. In addition, the colleges may admit — and are encouraged to do so — all persons over eighteen years of age who can profit from their instructional programs.

Admissions policies are sometimes defined in the enabling act which authorizes the institutions. For example, a section of the Illinois Public Junior College Act of 1965 has this stipulation: "The Class I junior college districts shall admit all students qualified to complete any one of their programs including general education, transfer, occupational, technical, and terminal, as long as space for effective instruction is available. After entry, the college shall counsel and distribute the students among its programs according to their interests and abilities."[4] In New York State similar policies are urged in the State University of New York's Master Plan goals: "These institutions [comprehensive community colleges] should be open to all high school graduates or persons with equivalent educational background. . . ."[5]

A major contribution of the community college to maintenance of educational opportunity is its growing commitment to offer its services to all persons, without regard to their previous educational experience or accomplishments, who can demonstrate that the educational programs available will be of value to them.

The open-door admissions policy is based upon the assumption that a much larger proportion of our population than is now doing so can benefit by education beyond the high school, and that the student can best show what he can do by being allowed to try. His efforts take place in an environment where alternative learning experiences are available to which he can turn within the same institution if they seem more suitable. This "chance to try" is provided by the community college at minimum cost, financially and socially, to the student and to the state.

A concomitant to nonselective admissions practices in the community college is greater selectivity by the university. This is a deliberate part of a state plan. For example, in California admission to the university is restricted to high school graduates who are in the upper 12 per cent of their class; the state colleges admit those in the upper 33⅓ per cent. Somewhat similar arrangements are being developed in other states. A university can be highly selective, and there are substantial arguments why it should be, if the total state program, through the community college, offers students who cannot qualify initially for the university the opportunity to continue their work. If they are successful in appropriate community college courses, the way is open to the university.

Variety of Programs

However, the educational role of the community college is much broader than that of preparing the student for the upper division of a four-year institution. This is not, in fact, its chief assignment. Its major task is to provide those learning experiences commonly needed as the level of educational effort in each community rises two years beyond the high school. Community colleges that limit their role to preparatory work for the four-year institutions will suffer from the same obvious inadequacies that have plagued high schools with similar proclivities in the past. The whole range of students to be served by the community institution must come under consideration. For more than half of the students the community college will represent final formal educational activity before they assume responsibilities of citizenship, family, and occupation. This means that their educational experiences, to be of greatest benefit, must have value in and of themselves, not just as preparation for either job or transfer. To offer only courses preparatory to other courses possibly to be taken at some dim future date is a fraud, even if accompanied by the best of intentions.

Right here is the crucial point in understanding the community college. For various reasons (among them some antipathy toward identification with secondary education), and drawn by the prestige attached to the college stereotype in our culture, the community college has leaned in the direction of higher education with its symbols, procedures, folklore, and objectives. No wonder, then, that the question is raised: "When is John Doe Community College going to become a regular college?" or that administrators and faculty are perplexed when a high proportion of its graduates do not transfer to a four-year college. The status it seeks has to be won on another basis because, in breadth of educational services, its assignment is similar now to that given another institution — the secondary school — a generation or two ago: to extend educational opportunity to all of the population. This carries with it the obligation for suitable arrangements both in the range of knowledge and in methods of instruction.

Occupational Education

Today there is a vast array of occupations for which at least two years of college study are necessary. Often referred to as "middle manpower" jobs, these semiprofessional and technical positions comprise a major category of employment in business, industry, and the professions. They are an outgrowth of the technological revolution, in which automation has combined with mechanization to replace the unskilled and even the skilled worker in many instances in factories, in offices, on farms, and in hospitals and laboratories. The national need for semiprofessional and technical manpower has been well documented. The community college not only prepares men and women for initial employment but provides programs to retrain and upgrade those who have been displaced from present jobs or forestalled in their advancement to better positions. Such efforts, incidentally, ought not to pose the alternative of technical *or* general education. Rather, they will interfuse the two. A national advisory committee put it this way:

> Neither does recognition of the need mean that a junior college program must be so exclusively vocational that it shuts out extension of cultural horizons or restricts adaptability to change. Time must be provided, even in a two-year curriculum, for at least basic courses in languages, arts and social sciences. The technicians of the future must be inoculated against the malady of over-specialization, a condition from which many professionals of the past suffered. They must not be forced to concentrate so narrowly on technology that they cannot be useful citizens or cannot accommodate to changes in their own specialties.[6]

In addition to two-year occupational programs, the community college also ordinarily offers programs with shorter time requirements — for example, preparation of licensed vocational nurses.

Further consideration of the growing importance of occupational education and community services will be found in subsequent chapters.

College Parallel

Beyond doubt, an important part of the community college program is similar to what is offered in the first two years in a four-year institution. Frequently called "college parallel," this work, if successfully completed, enables the student to move to the four-year college with just two years to go for attainment of the bachelor's degree. All states with educational plans which include the community college require it to have this function. As previously indicated, with the larger proportion of baccalaureate-bound students taking their first two years in the community college, some universities have cut back on their lower-division enrollments in favor of increasing the proportion of students at the upper-division and graduate levels. And in Florida, New York, and Illinois, new public universities have been established that have no lower division and look to the community colleges, accordingly, as a major source of students.

How many community college students do transfer to four-year colleges? In California about 20 per cent of the entering students eventually transfer, and about 80 per cent of these are granted a four-year degree. Approximately thirty out of every hundred entering freshmen in Florida transfer to four-year colleges. This proportion has held consistently over the past several years.

Community college students characteristically will declare, upon enrollment, that they intend to go on to a four-year college — nationally about two-thirds state this intention. However, one-third actually do transfer, according to the latest research of the Center for Research and Development in Higher Education at the University of California.[7] Although this is a fraction of the total enrollments, it still represents a large number of students and is increasing substantially each year. Both the community colleges and the four-year institutions must take this fact into account in their planning.

A perennial problem for the community college in organizing courses that will carry transfer credit is the great affection each four-year college has for the presumed uniqueness of the content, sequence, and titles of its courses. Obviously, no community college could duplicate the programs offered by the hundreds of institutions to which its graduates might transfer. There would be little vitality in community college curriculums, moreover, if subject matter, textbooks, and course organization were prescribed by the senior colleges. The aim, therefore, is toward course equivalence. In a number of states the four-year institutions have agreed to give full credit for courses successfully completed which, though not identical, are equivalent to those offered in their own lower divisions. Incidentally, the university's concern is not limited to the community college transfer. A recent study showed that transfer is more prevalent among four-year colleges than between the community college and the four-year institution. Transfer students today find that they have plenty of company at most universities.

To assure that those who have the aptitude and achievement to qualify for it do have education beyond the community college, the latter must prepare students for *successful* work in the upper divisions. The Public Junior College Act in Illinois is very specific: "Students allowed entry to college transfer programs must have ability and competence similar to that possessed by students admitted to state universities for similar programs. Entry level competence to such college transfer programs may be achieved through successful completion of other preparatory courses offered by the college."[8]

In this connection, Knoell and Medsker, in their important study of the transfer student, recommend that weak students with both subject matter and scholarship deficiencies remain in the community college for more than two years before transfer in order to catch up with their classmates who began junior college without deficiencies. They observe, too, that the student who stays in the junior college for his full two years tends to be more successful when he transfers.

A large percentage of university and college graduates in states where the community college is well established now begin their work in community colleges. How well do they do? According to Knoell and Medsker, ". . . at least 75 per cent and probably as high as 80 per cent of the junior college transfer students achieved their degree objectives during a four-year period which began with their transfer to a four-year college or university in 1960."[9] Characteristically the student's grade point average in his first term after transfer drops below his cumulative junior college averages but shows continuing improvement in succeeding terms. This "transfer shock" can be eased by the efforts of both sending and receiving institutions to provide for effective relationships in regard to curricula, counseling, financial aid, and to assure the matching of the transfer student with the proper upper-division institution.

The question about how well the student does has an important corollary: how well do the colleges do, both two-year and four-year? Knoell and Medsker found that judgments could not be made about the performance of the students independent of the context of the colleges in which they were enrolled and of the state systems of which they were a part. "All or most junior college students could be successful in achieving their degree goals after transfer if they would select four-year institutions and major fields which are appropriate to their ability and prior achievement."[10]

Obviously two-year and four-year colleges need to know each other better than has been true before. This begins with the understanding that the community college allows increasing numbers of high school graduates to begin work for the bachelor's degree who would not otherwise be able to do so for reasons of academic or economic deficiency, or for lack of family encouragement. Whatever institutional arrangements are devised for passage of the student from one institution to another, the aim must be to facilitate his progress, not to impede it. In an increasing number of states there exists both a spirit and organization through which this can be accomplished.

The importance of transferring to the institution which is "right" for the student introduces another essential service of the community college: student personnel work. In the words of Professor T. R. McConnell of the University of California:

Community colleges, therefore, have assumed the enormously difficult task of educating highly diversified student bodies. It is obvious that these institutions must provide highly differentiated educational programs. It should be equally clear that if students are to choose wisely among many different courses and curricula leading to a great variety of future careers, they must be assisted in identifying their abilities and aptitudes, in assessing their deficiencies and their potentialities, and in rationalizing their aspirations.[11]

Community college students have choices to make. Their first decision is behind them — to enter the college. But what program of study shall they pursue? Assistance is needed not only in viewing the array of possibilities but in taking a self-inventory. Sometimes aspirations require a cooling though not defeating touch of realism. In other instances the student needs help to see that his capacities are greater than he has come to believe. There is a moving about in the community college, an exploration of fields of knowledge and experience, an examination of options. Then decisions must be made, tentative and open to review. No comprehensive community college can perform its functions as an open-door institution unless it offers highly skilled and professional student personnel services and they are being used. These run the gamut from counseling to testing to placement.

The Problem of Insufficient Educational Background

Among the students will very probably be some who have experienced denial of achievement in the past, possibly because of faulty or inadequate educational services. No one knows how many youth and adults with similar problems never get this far, to their detriment as well as that of the nation. One of the most persuasive arguments for doing something about this problem came a short time ago, not from a professional educator but from the former Secretary of Defense. Secretary McNamara described a plan for the military services to use advanced techniques to train up to 100,000 of the 600,000 each year who are rejected for physical or educational reasons. "The 32 million Americans who are poor were not born without intellectual potential," he said. "They were not brain-poor at birth; but only privilege-poor, advantage-poor, opportunity-poor." Many fail the aptitude or achievement tests, he pointed out, because "these tests are geared to the psychology of traditional, formal, classroom, teacher-paced instruction" and because the cultural environment of the test takers "is radically different from that assumed by the test-designers."

"Clearly the way to measure [a man's] aptitude," he went on, "is to place him in a situation that offers the encouragement he has never had before. That means a good teacher and a good course of instruction, well supported by self-paced, audio-visual aids. It also means less formal, classroom, theoretical instruction, and more practical on-the-job training."[12]

Secretary McNamara described what must be the attitude and methodology of the community college if it is to distinguish itself by responding to critical societal needs that other institutions "cannot or will not meet." Various names are given to this function: remedial, repair, salvage, developmental. Often there is more than a hint of disparagement. But it is a legitimate — even more, an essential — task of the community college to deal with inadequacies in the student's educational background. Professionals in our society straighten teeth, prescribe glasses, suggest exercises for the flabby and diets for the obese. The professionals of the community college will be qualified both in competence and in attitude to assist students who come with handicaps and who, in the language of a recent report, "cannot progress in any type of collegiate training until they first achieve better mastery of tool subjects or the symbol systems: reading, composition, listening, speech, fundamental logic, arithmetic."[13]

Community college leaders know that "remediation" is an inescapable obligation in an institution which has an open-door admissions policy and which invites enrollment of all high school graduates and others who can benefit from its programs. But how to do this? This is the biting question that is under widespread and sometimes agonizing discussion. A number of institutions are highly committed to the search for more effective arrangements for learning and are leaving no aspect of the college operations unexamined. Among their discoveries is that the inexperienced instructor is the one most often found in a remedial classroom. Yet the teacher is the most important element in the success of remedial programs. "It is ironic that inexperienced teachers are sometimes considered unprepared to serve on major committees but yet are given one of the most difficult teaching assignments."[14]

It has been suggested that qualified elementary teachers be employed in some institutions to teach students in remedial courses since they are not handicapped by subject matter specialization and the status terms "college material" and "college level" may have little meaning to them when accepting teaching assignment.

The "system" is not beyond scrutiny as it affects definitions of achievement. At Laney College in California the faculty believe that the present grading practices are punitive. They are planning a grading system of A, B, C and W (Withdraw) only. They feel that the investment of time in a course without satisfactory completion of the material is punishment enough; a student will not be penalized with a D or an F for failure, but will simply be allowed to repeat the course.

New approaches are being tried under careful research conditions in such colleges as those in Bakersfield, Compton, Contra Costa, and Los Angeles in California, and Forest Park Community College in St. Louis. These experiments are described in a recent publication on remedial education in the community junior college. The author calls for more careful investigation of this kind:

> "In addition to experimentation with certain variation in program planning and development, more experimentation is needed to determine the place and value of large-class and small-class instruction, team teaching, lay assistance, technological aid, and programmed instruction — experimentation developed to facilitate individualized teaching so that each student's program could

be designed with attention to what he already knows and needs to learn rather than accommodating the mythical remedial student."[15]

Little wonder that Professor McConnell calls the work of the community college "the enormously difficult task of educating highly diversified student bodies," or that there are occasional tendencies for community college personnel to look with some envy toward institutions with a bit more homogeneity.

Coordination with Other Institutions

The community college has its assignment within an organization of education which requires a distinct division of labor if it is to be effective. Statements from California and New York support this assertion:

> But the junior colleges are particularly charged with providing services and programs not offered by other institutions and to educate a more heterogeneous student body.
>
> Two-year and four-year colleges, in a planned, coordinated, and complete system of public higher education, provide essential and complementary, but distinctive services in post-high school education.

In a number of cities where public universities exist the question has been raised, Is there need for a community college? That question has been answered in the affirmative in a number of places in recognition of two kinds of educational institutions with different and essential and complementary services. Gainesville, Florida, has the University of Florida and Santa Fe Junior College. At East Lansing, Michigan, there are Lansing Community College and Michigan State University. In Seattle, where the University of Washington is located, Seattle Community College has recently been established. Just getting under way is a public junior college in Champaign-Urbana, Illinois, home of the University of Illinois.

One of the latest examples of an institutional partnership to meet educational needs can be found in Cleveland. Cuyahoga Community College, the first community college in Ohio, opened its doors in 1962 and already has more than 10,000 students. In accordance with the master plan for higher education in Ohio, the comprehensive Cleveland State University has now been established in that city. Under the leadership of the two boards and the presidents, it has been agreed that CSU and CCC serve different purposes and different clienteles and complement each other. A five-point program has been developed to coordinate the work of the two institutions. The major section of the plan calls for rapid development of the community college as a center for freshman and sophomore courses. It also proposes a wide range of two-year technical and occupational programs in business, electronics, health, and social services. The university presumably will continue its freshman and sophomore programs on a limited basis but will concentrate on building strong upper-division programs and high-quality graduate and professional schools.

The institutions will work together to develop joint counseling services so that each student selects the program as well as the institution for which he is best fitted. Efforts will also be pooled in making enrollment projections and in fact gathering and analysis. A joint council has been suggested, which will meet regularly to explore the possibilities of increased cooperation. An editorial in the *Cleveland Press* comments that the proposals for cooperation and the educational leadership demonstrated "should dispel the apprehensions of those who feared the two schools might develop as competitors instead of allies."

The community college is a social invention designed to play its part within the nation's whole program of education. It has evolved to meet new educational needs and to supplement and complement services provided by other institutions. It should not attempt to be a university; nor, for that matter, is society well served if the university tries to be a community college. The roles are different. Each institution is needed. Each will be judged in terms of how well it does the job for which it was established.

In short, our society needs the whole bag of clubs (to borrow a golf term). The design of each club is determined by its function. All the clubs are useful in the game — and the more expert the player, the more clubs he can use. They have some similarities, but the putter has little merit when compared with the wedge in getting the ball out of the rough, and a driver is an awkward instrument at best for putting. The driver is used for the tee and the putter on the green. Which has most prestige? Which is of greatest value? Should we pound the putter to make it a wedge and improve our game? Obviously, each club is needed. Each is meant for a different situation. No service is performed by making them alike. The value of the club or boat or automobile or college depends on how effectively it performs in the situation for which it was designed. Community college advocates, in their understandable concern about prestige for their institutions, ought to be willing to settle for this.

NOTES

[1] UNESCO, *Access to Higher Education,* statement by C. K. Zurayk in Foreword to Volume I by Frank Bowles. New York: International Documents Service, Columbia University Press, 1963.

[2] Richard Pearson, "The Challenge of Curricular Change." New York: College Entrance Examination Board, 1966.

[3] Robert J. Havighurst, "Junior College Student Personnel Programs — Appraisal and Development," report to Carnegie Corporation of New York from the National Committee for Appraisal and Development of Junior College Student Personnel Programs, November 1965.

[4] Ernest F. Anderson and James S. Spencer, "Report of Selected Data and Characteristics — Illinois Public Junior Colleges, 1966–67." Springfield: Illinois Junior College Board, 1967.

[5] "The Comprehensive Community College: A Policy Statement of the New York State Board of Regents," Albany, February 27, 1967.

[6] Statement by the National Advisory Committee on the Junior College, "A National Resource for Occupational Education," Washington: American Association of Junior Colleges, December 1964.

[7] Dale Tillery, Center for Research and Development in Higher Education, University of California, Berkeley, statement to the author, 1967.

[8] Anderson and Spencer, *op. cit.*

[9] Dorothy M. Knoell and Leland L. Medsker, *From Junior to Senior College: A National Study of the Transfer Student.* Washington: American Council on Education, 1965.

[10] *Ibid.*

[11] Charles C. Collins, *Junior College Student Personnel Programs — What They Are and What They Should Be.* Washington: American Association of Junior Colleges, 1967.

[12] Robert S. McNamara, speech before the Veterans of Foreign Wars, New York, August 23, 1966.

[13] Collins, *op. cit.*

[14] John E. Rouche, "Salvage, Redirection, or Custody?" ERIC Clearinghouse for Junior College Information, monograph series. Washington: American Association of Junior Colleges, 1968.

[15] *Ibid.*

4

THE TWO-THIRDS WHO WILL NOT TRANSFER

Does not our present pattern, which involves a
high-prestige value for the bachelor's degree, postpone
too long entry into a significant career for many youths?
I suggest that all who are responsible for employment
policy consider emphasizing the two-year associate
of arts degree and de-emphasizing the B.A.

— James B. Conant, *Saturday Review*
January 13, 1968

Ω ne out of three students enrolled in the community college will continue his work in a four-year college. The other two will not. What are the community colleges doing about the other two students?

They are doing a great deal but not nearly enough. The question arises out of data which carry the impact but also the shortcomings of many generalizations. The impact: Community college programs and procedures often are based upon the assumption that most students will transfer. Since the assumption is not supported by the facts, neither are the educational structures that are built upon it. The shortcoming: The experience reported is nationwide in scope; therefore it is unlikely to hold true for any single institution. One more caveat: No one knows whether the student will be in the one-third or the two-thirds until after the fact — that is, until he transfers or does not. And it is the aim of the community college to keep open the student's educational options as long as possible.

National studies over several years show that as many as two-thirds of the students declare their intention to work toward the bachelor's degree when they enroll in the community college. They do not expect to terminate their academic pursuits with graduation from that institution and certainly not short of that. But actually two-thirds of those enrolling will *not* transfer to a four-year college. They will require organized educational experiences other than those leading to the bachelor's degree. It does not follow that they are therefore "dropouts," weak in persistence, or that they are not successful in achieving some personal and educational objectives. For them, however, and for that matter for as many as two-thirds of the high school graduates, the conventional bachelor's degree may not be an appropriate target — at least not immediately after high school. Other educational programs may be more suitable.

New Occupations

What kinds of programs should they be? A substantial part of the two-thirds will prepare for employment. They need jobs. And they have found that the level of skills and understanding represented in high school graduation is not enough. Occupational education is a major function of the comprehensive community college. In terms of numbers served it may become the foremost curricular function. A remarkable variety of programs is developing. They reflect both a great range of student interests and aptitudes and requirements for personnel by new occupations in our complex society.

Events taking place in the health fields are an impressive illustration of what may happen in other occupations:

> The lone practitioner of medicine is an anachronism, as is his counterpart in other professions. The knowledge explosion has overwhelmed the professional and escalated his responsibilities. Increasingly he analyzes, plans, and administers services which are provided by others — others to whom he delegates in large measure routines carried out under his direction. The "others" are technicians and assistants. In medicine and dentistry, the list of supporting technicians is long. Some of the names are well known — such as medical laboratory technicians, x-ray technicians, opticians, inhalation therapy technicians, and dental hygienists. Others, many others, are doing the work, but their role as medical and dental assistants is less well developed. For some we even lack names. They not only assist the physician and the dentist, but, in this expanding field of knowledge and service, there is need for technical assistance for the professional nurse, the physical and occupational therapist, the medical record librarian, the dietitian, and many others.[1]

What has this to do with community colleges? Health authorities urge that they offer programs like these:

Dental Assisting
Dental Laboratory Technology
Environmental Health
   Technology
Inhalation Therapy
   Technology
Medical Office Assisting
Medical Record Technology
Ophthalmic Dispensing

Mental Health Technology
Radioisotope Technology
Nursing
X-Ray Technology
Occupational Therapy Assisting
Prosthetics-Orthotics
   Technology
Medical Emergency
   Technology

Semiprofessional Positions

As the nation becomes more urban, the problems and possibilities of the cities call for new patterns of preparation for jobs, some with descriptions yet to be written. The community college is looked to for semiprofessional personnel:

> In recent months the American Society of Planning Officials has received considerable evidence that local government agencies concerned with planning, housing, urban renewal, code enforcement, traffic and highways, environmental health, and other urban problems, are in need of trained personnel to perform jobs at the semi-professional level. The need is particularly great in planning agencies. . . . We would urge that junior colleges be informed of the enormous potential for career opportunities in planning and urban development offices, the types of skills required, and the suggested curriculum for this type of career. . . . A corollary need which we would like to give attention to would be an analysis and identification of the variety of tasks that could be performed by semi-professional personnel (even though now performed by professionals) and preparation of "model" job descriptions, classifications, titles, and salary levels.[2]

Already under way in some institutions are curriculums to prepare semiprofessional personnel to assist city planners and urban renewal professionals. Feasibility studies are in process for programs in land-use surveys and studies, code enforcement, housing inspection, and traffic control.

Nearly two hundred community colleges cooperate with police departments to offer two-year associate degree programs to prepare police officers. City planning, highway safety technology, and social work are other illustrations of the occupational needs in public service to which the community college is responding.

Public Services

In America the hospitality industry, as it is called, is vast and expanding. During the past two decades the need for trained personnel to work in hotels, motels, institutions, and food service operations has been increasing at a tremendous rate. Programs are offered in community colleges in food service management and hotel and restaurant operations. As is true in many other fields, these include internships or on-the-job and cooperative experiences.

Large chain retail stores and community colleges have combined efforts to prepare personnel in sales and department management. Science and industry, including the newly important fields of space and marine sciences, have expressed urgent requirements for technicians in research as well as in engineering.

An advertisement in the *Wall Street Journal* carried this message: "St. Louis Grows in the Strategic Center of America — New Junior College to Meet Industry's Manpower Needs. The growing manpower needs of industry and business will have a new and continuing source of technicians and skilled men and women." The ad was placed by a large utility, Union Electric.

The chairman of the U.S. Civil Service Commission, John W. Macy, Jr., announced recently: "A new 'career highway' into the federal service has been opened by the United States Civil Service Commission, and the go signal is on for junior college graduates. . . . The new program is aimed directly at the junior college graduate and persons with equivalent combinations of education and experience."[3] According to Commissioner Macy, this is a "new recognition by the federal government that the junior colleges are turning out trained personnel of great potential value to the nation's largest (and one of its best) employers."

Values of Occupational Education

Industry, science, business, public service, and health — the changing world of occupations has met up with the community college and found a source of qualified personnel. Granted that this situation is of great benefit to the employers as well as to the welfare of the nation. What are the values to the students aside from the obvious one of landing a job? What case can be made for the advantages of an occupational program?

That the graduate can get a job, and a job that is related to his interests and training, is no little thing. Not only does it provide him with income and society with essential services, but in our culture what a person does (his occupation) has a great deal to do with who he is (his sense of identity).

Motivation for many students is increased when they can look forward to employment and the opportunities to use what they are learning in a year or two rather than in an indefinite and somewhat hazy future.

A large proportion of community college students are inclined toward the practical and applied rather than the theoretical and abstract. They need a sense of contact with the "real world," not a simulated one of words and symbols. Action-oriented occupational programs with experience on the job can capture their interest whereas immersion in a highly verbal atmosphere can defeat them. This does not mean that occupational students learn no linguistic skills or lack the ability to theorize. But in emphasis and sequence the application of knowledge and skills development come first.

There is another potential value in occupational education. Skills requirements not only might change but almost surely will change. Jobs become obsolete. Beyond skills, however, there are learning residuals — attitudes, values, and social competence — in well-conceived occupational programs. The knowledge of how to size up a problem, collect the pertinent information, decide among alternatives, communicate with associates, evaluate results, record them for the information and understanding of others, correct errors, improve procedures, and accept responsibility comes remarkably close to that often associated with standard liberal education.

Problems Facing Occupational Education

The reader might be inclined to say here: "Both the student and our society apparently benefit by the services of the community college in preparing people for occupations. The point has been made. These institutions are performing a valuable public service." But actually, the picture is not that bright. While the potential is there, the practice is less than perfect. Some of the reasons are rooted in broad cultural attitudes. Others stem from the attitudes of the educational profession.

The problem begins with an enthusiasm in our society for the "upper" (white-collar) occupations, emphasizing the professional and managerial categories and consequently giving lower status to other occupational categories. In a nation which encourages aspiration and puts its faith in economic and social mobility, there is nothing wrong with this — if a person can indeed qualify for the presumably greater responsibilities at the top of the ladder and if society can use him. Realistically, however, one must face the fact of an almost infinite variety of human talent and a bewildering array of societal tasks. It is to be hoped that talents and tasks can be linked up. Among the most urgent obligations of education is that of removing the handicaps that interfere with this process.

When a leading statesman of Kenya said, "Our young people are afflicted with academic disease," he was describing the same dilemma. "All of our young people want to be political scientists and philosophers and statesmen, whether or not they have the necessary aptitudes and abilities. Furthermore," he said, "this country needs surveyors, and secretaries, and nurses, and mechanics, and we need many more of these than we do of the others."

A similar problem exists in our big cities. Community colleges established there during the past several years were expected to draw into their occupational programs many students from economically depressed areas. The results have been disappointing. Enrollments were small. Those students apparently were not convinced that occupational education would help them up the economic and social ladder.

There is no question that a major problem confronting occupational education is its comparative lack of prestige. However, assuming that a higher proportion of high school graduates ought to enter occupational programs, some things can be done to make the programs more inviting.

A real gain will have been registered when the student sees that these programs prepare for job *entry*. A lifelong commitment is not called for. He is making a beginning, and his future course is open ended. He is not undertaking a "terminal program." Other educational and training opportunities will be available to him as he wants to move up in his field or move out and into something else. A national committee urged recently that the educational system be loosened up so that the student could leave when other activities seemed more rewarding and could return when he was ready for further study:

> Education, training, and re-training should be available to individuals throughout their lives. . . . A system of education that is open ended, with freedom for mature students to enter, leave when alternative experiences seem more fruitful, and then re-enter, can be a reality through the coordinated efforts of public schools, community colleges, vocational schools, universities, and employers.[4]

If curriculum planners can devise programs that are not only open ended but broadly based, the student can move about in his field as his interests and objectives change. To satisfy this requirement and at the same time make sure that the student is well equipped to enter his field of work is a difficult assignment. Experimentation is under way, however, in a number of fields, including health, to establish core curriculums. A cluster of related technologies may have a common year of study, specialization coming the second year. An arrangement of this kind gives the student more mobility during the period in which he is sharpening his objectives. Also, retraining for other occupations or adaptation to advances in his present occupation is facilitated by a broader base of preparation.

Occupational education in the community college will be more inviting if faculty, counselors, and parents avoid equating (sometimes unconsciously) "transfer" with "good student," and "occupational" with "poor student." From high school days on, the student picks up clues in his environment that suggest the inferiority of the occupational student as compared with his baccalaureate-bound colleague. "Bill is a weak student. An occupational program is about as much as he can handle." Bill may very well be a weak student and need help, but to consign him to occupational education is not the answer. There may be a *program* within occupational education which is right for him, but the field in general requires as wide a spectrum of aptitudes and abilities as is called for by the transfer program — possibly wider.

Differentiating between occupational and transfer students on the basis of generalized ability is a disservice to the student and attaches an unwarranted and inaccurate label to the entire field. Some occupational programs place a premium on manual or manipulative or communication skills. Others may require academic abilities quite similar to those of the transfer liberal arts student. Not only different areas of study but different levels of programs call for different capabilities. Occupational education is a broad and complex field. Too many educators have viewed it from a distance, with a consequent lack of detail. They need to examine it at closer range and to see its parts and relationships.

ATTITUDE OF THE EDUCATIONAL COMMUNITY

In fact it is in the educational community itself that occupational education finds its most vexatious problems. Here, in long-standing concepts, definitions, academic structures, and prestige symbols, lies the most resistance to the full emergence of occupational education in the community college. Some of the resistance resides within the institution itself; some in its relationships with high schools and universities.

Let us consider the high schools first. With all of the advantages of proximity, very few community colleges have done an effective job in relating to these institutions. In stressing their identity as something different from the high schools, they have neglected possibilities for joint efforts which could be of marked benefit to the student.

Better communication would encourage high school counselors to discuss with their students the merits of occupational programs as well as of the more familiar college sequences. High schools welcome college and university recruiters. Spokesmen for occupational curriculums are needed to give information about the advantages, rewards, and requirements of these community college programs which lead directly to employment.

Program articulation possibilities have been barely glanced at. There are potentially great advantages to the student in a three- or four-year technical or semiprofessional curriculum which brackets the last years of the high school and the two years of community college. This is only one suggestion. Both the high schools and the community college need to exploit the resource of their proximity.

Another "family" relationship needs cultivation: that with the universities. Much has been done in articulation between two-year and four-year institutions in order to facilitate transfer of students. But little attention has been given to the equally important necessity of mutual understanding of the occupational programs of community colleges. University professors in general have been more interested in the professional than in the semiprofessional, in the scientist than in the technician, in addition to knowledge than in application of knowledge. Within the university these preoccupations must dominate. Yet in addition, the community college, with a vast and new assignment in American education, surely must become a legitimate university concern and an object of service.

Few community colleges are located beyond easy travel distance of a university. As a result, it has been possible in some parts of the country for universities and clusters of community colleges to join in a continuing relationship for purposes of institutional research, curriculum development, and staff preparation. The result has been not only improved curriculums and more competent personnel but a high quality of interaction — travel in both directions — and consequently more effective communication. However, a much greater scale of effort is called for. Talented people from the universities need to join with those of the community college and occupational fields to devise both improved and new curriculums in these rapidly changing educational fields. A prototype of the university interest required can be found in the new approaches to mathematics and physics and languages formulated during the past decade.

Keeping Pace with Changes in Occupational Fields

The pace of change poses real problems for occupational education. How can teachers keep up? What assurance is there that programs are realistic? By what means do counselors keep current about occupational trends and requirements? A study of community colleges showed that institutions with the best student personnel services were weakest in occupational counseling and placement. Both of these services represent points of contact with real-life employment conditions. A gap of varying but always troublesome proportions exists between the educational experiences of the student in the classroom or shop and the requirements of the job into which he is moving.

The faculty are not unaware of this difficulty. They have identified as their greatest concern the depletion of their "intellectual capital." For the teacher in occupational fields this means knowledge of the requirements, changes, concepts, personnel, and literature in his field. His intellectual capital needs replenishment. The chances are that he is not able to maintain it. At present there is no overall systematic and organized arrangement by which the community college is kept tuned in to changes in the occupational fields. Nevertheless, some institutions, separately or in groups, have adopted promising measures and are planning others.

One way to stay current is through expansion of work experience programs. The community college, usually located in the city, has a built-in asset in its proximity to the occupational life of the community. The fact that its students characteristically work part time (estimates suggest that as many as 60 per cent have jobs) provides a running start toward an arrangement which relates their jobs to their training. But beyond these factors that favor a combination of classroom and on-the-job experience, there is the added value to the institution of a daily testing of its programs by the actual work setting. "Feedback," prompt and realistic, can impel indicated changes.

Two devices commonly used in academic circles could reduce the problem of lag between the occupational classroom and actual job conditions: visiting scientist arrangements and exchanges. Under foundation grants outstanding scientists have visited colleges and universities to lecture and consult on the latest developments in their fields. They have also, upon request, examined courses offered by an institution which were in their field of competence and commented on the suitability of facilities and equipment. Business, industry, government, and health interests would benefit along with the community college if plans were made more often for competent personnel from those areas to visit it. Two or three days or perhaps even a full semester could be spent in residence at one institution or in shared time with several institutions.

Turn this proposal around the other way: Employers could provide summer working opportunities or leave-of-absence employment so that faculty and counselors could have frequent and meaningful experience in the fields for which they are preparing personnel.

Another way to reduce the barriers between educational institutions and occupations is suggested by experience in the health sphere. Community colleges prepare nurses, using the clinical facilities of the hospitals in the area. There is no need for the institution to duplicate the physical setting in which its students will be employed; for many reasons that would be poor policy. This approach has worked and justifies adaptation to other occupational fields. Not only will the college find economic and educational benefits in utilizing facilities of hospitals, department stores, factories, government offices, and aircraft plants, but the occupational programs it offers are more likely to be in step with changes in those fields.

A teacher in occupational education has a difficult assignment. He must be at home in the shop or laboratory or clinic and in the classroom. His competence must be as highly respected by the engineer, or physician, or businessman as by his students. To make this dual existence possible, however, changes in organization and procedures will be required of both the occupational world and the community college.

INTERFACULTY COORDINATION

There is another element in which some changes may or may not be necessary: the community college faculty. The comprehensive institution is seriously handicapped in its broad mission unless the faculty strives toward the peer relationship which results when each appreciates the worth of the others' fields of knowledge, whether it be social science, X-ray technology, or automobile mechanics. This relationship is easier proposed than activated. The "academic disease" referred to previously is not totally unknown in faculty circles. Sometimes a frame of reference borrowed from the liberal arts college or university is used in judging the values of the college programs and hence of the people who represent them. Most faculty members had their first contact with the community college when they reported for their teaching assignment. Their student days were spent in liberal arts colleges and universities. They are the products of the graduate schools of the universities. They obviously may bring with them the status symbols, the philosophy, the concepts of the university or college. On the other hand, industry, business, and government are the backgrounds of faculty in the occupational programs. They probably have a bachelor's degree and often a master's degree, but they may possess a different set of status symbols and concepts of the goals and methods of education.

Integration of the many parts of the comprehensive institution begins right here, with the faculty. No matter how profound the policy statements of the board or the president, the actual character of the college will be determined in time by the teacher in the classroom and laboratory. Success of the comprehensive open-door community college hangs on the extent to which the faculty accept that concept and on that value framework construct suitable patterns of faculty organization, bases for faculty distinction, and judgments of worth about the college programs.

Judging and Fulfilling Needs

One of the judgments to be made by faculty and administration concerns the breadth and variety of occupational programs. Obviously no institution can or ought to offer everything. Feasibility studies are essential to a determination of need and resources. The services of other institutions must be taken into account. In metropolitan areas such as Los Angeles and Chicago some programs are available in all the seven or eight colleges in the community college district. Others are offered in only one or two. Comprehensiveness is achieved by pooling the institutional curriculums. A statewide approach is made in New York in the case of highly specialized programs. For example, only one institution serves the fashion industry, the Fashion Institute of Technology.

The more urgent question before America's community colleges today is, Are we doing enough? Are the occupational programs diversified enough to deliver on the expectations encouraged by the open-door institution? One competent observer says that they are not: "Many junior colleges continue to invite students into the open door whom they are not prepared to educate and for whom they do not have either proper programs or guidance. These students leave in large numbers very early after entering the institution and should be seen as 'push outs' rather than 'drop outs.' "[5]

Community colleges can be placed within commuting distance of almost everybody. It is to be hoped that they can continue to be operated with low cost to the students. But if their services do not possess sufficient reach, these institutions may still default on their promise.

Some will suggest that there is a recognized collegiate "menu," and "if they want it they can come and get it and if they don't like it they don't have to eat it." This attitude conveys the notion that the menu is selected by the cook to suit his liking and that it is neither his pleasure nor his duty to whet the appetite and consult the tastes of his guests. But it *is* the duty and ought to be the pleasure of those in education to reach more people than have been served before with opportunities suitable in content and method so that they learn to support themselves, to contribute toward society's corporate life, and to develop social perspective and compassion.

When a community college commits itself to occupational education, it is doing much more than adding some courses that prepare for employment. It is affirming an institutional viewpoint which affects every aspect of its operations. In its breadth of programs, its counseling, and its teaching process it is taking a position about education and the people who should be involved in it.

NOTES

[1] Robert E. Kinsinger, *Education for Health Technicians — An Overview.* Washington: American Association of Junior Colleges, 1965.

[2] Dennis O'Harrow, Executive Director, American Society of Planning Officials, Chicago, letter to the author.

[3] John W. Macy, Jr., "We Want Junior Federal Assistants," *Junior College Journal,* February 1967.

[4] National Commission on Technology, Automation, and Economic Progress, *Technology and the American Economy.* Washington: U.S. Government Printing Office, 1966.

[5] Dale, Tillery, Center for Research and Development in Higher Education, University of California, Berkeley, letter to the author, June 12, 1967.

5

A COLLEGE FOR
THE COMMUNITY

Clearly the educational need of these times is not only that education have the unified approach appropriate to communal life, but that communities be developed in which such education is possible. The community, in other words, is both ends and means in education. It is, or should be, the primary context of human growth and education. Here the development of the individual and society in their long courses of interfused behavior should take place.

— Baker Brownell, *Human Community*
Harper and Brothers, 1950

The community college is not just for the "kids." Nor is its field of service bounded by the parking lots. Rather, it is an educational resource center in which age is no object, and the district is its campus.

Not long ago a person's education was thought to be ended at graduation from high school or college. Some institutions made this plain; they were "finishing schools." Graduation or "commencement" ceremonies intimated that the student was to put down the instruments of learning and move out into the world. The faculty were insistent that prescribed amounts of material be covered and therefore available to the graduate for meeting the unknown problems which lay ahead. That the information conveyed might in time prove to be incomplete, inaccurate, or dead wrong did not deter the view that "if you don't get it now, you'll never have another chance."

In this regard we are somewhat wiser. We know that everything cannot be learned in two years or four years, or twelve plus four. The expanding and changing properties of knowledge as well as the variable needs and interests of the learner call for a concept of lifelong learning and hence continuous opportunity for education. In the future, therefore, educational services and facilities will be as convenient as gasoline service stations. When a person needs fuel in order to generate the means to reach his next destination, the opportunity will be at hand.

Just as each community now has its elementary and secondary schools for children and youth, so each will have its center for continuing education, the community college. Close by, with low cost to the student, and diversified in its offerings, this in-

82

stitution performs one of its most important functions through service to the residents of its area throughout their lives.

A Center for Continuing Education

As a person grows older what he wants from the college will change as his concerns and responsibilities change. Soon after high school he may study to prepare for employment or for transfer to the university. After he goes to work, he finds that through a course in personnel administration he can qualify for a better position. Later he joins others to request a seminar on the latest developments in tax laws as they apply to his business. He becomes interested in boating and takes a course in small boat handling. He decides to run for public office and needs a refresher course in American government.

Perhaps his wife took two years at the community college and transferred to the university for a bachelor's degree in liberal arts. She wants a job for a while before they have children. Secretaries are needed in the city. An intensive one-semester program provides her with the skills needed to secure employment. Later the children come, and she looks to the college again for a course in child or adolescent psychology. A class in consumer economics helps her in the financial management of the home. She wants to know more about the pros and cons of the Vietnam war, so she enrolls in an evening class on Southeast Asia and its crucial issues.

These are illustrations of the use made of the college by its district residents. Objectives vary greatly: work toward a degree at one stage; vocational proficiency at another; satisfaction of a desire to learn at any time. The above sample of the educational requirements two people may have during their lives indicates the directions in which the college should respond in an organized way.

A learning resources center of this kind, to be used by people of all ages who can profit by instruction, bears little resemblance to the institution that adds a few evening courses to its "regular" daytime schedule for the benefit of adults. All the courses are considered regular. All the students are adults although of varying ages. The only significant change brought about by the setting sun is that the lights are turned on; the evening hours are a bona fide part of the college day.

Such an institution requires programs, facilities, and procedures that fit its mission. It will gear its arrangements to the adult. Nothing can cool the ardor for learning more quickly than time-consuming encounters with administrative red tape or with requirements and procedures pitched to the assumed maturity level of the adolescent.

The college will not be a domain exclusively of youth during the day and of older students at night. Opportunities for study will be available at the convenience of the student — and, of course, within the limits of institutional feasibility. However, these limits often need testing and in fact can be greatly stretched. Miami-Dade Junior College showed how through its Weekend College. Initiated in 1965, Weekend College offers a full associate degree program in Saturday-only classes. It was designed especially for the many would-be students kept out of the college classroom by time or circumstance:

> The rigors of all-day classes, scheduled in three-hour blocks, failed to daunt the highly motivated Saturday scholars, and an initial enrollment of 328 grew to 356 by year's end. Of all ages and diverse walks of life, they included housewives who had baby-sitter problems except on Saturday when fathers were at home, men prevented from regular day or night classes by irregular business hours, working wives whose office-plus-home duties left no time to spare during the work week, and many others.[1]

Essex Community College in Baltimore evolved a program to attract senior citizens (over sixty) into the classrooms. They were admitted as auditors, tuition free, providing there was room in the particular class for them. The college waived all of its usual entrance examinations but interviewed each applicant for admission. City and county commissions on problems of the aging joined with the college in the view that continued education was one of the answers to the problem of mental deterioration among the elderly.

Some community colleges have passed with flying colors the supreme test of adaptability. They have scheduled courses for employees coming off the night shift in large industrial firms.

Suiting Students' Convenience

Few college plants are built for this kind of student body — people of all ages who come and go both day and night. The facilities need to convey the philosophy that this institution has a commitment to all of its students, nocturnal and diurnal. At night it must be as inviting and safe and lively as during the day, and there must be complete availability of library, bookstore, food service, physical education facilities, and registration and counseling offices. A California community college shows its equal regard for the students after 5:00 P.M. Before that hour, which is usually associated with the close of the working day in America, 5,955 students are enrolled in classes; in the evening hours the number is 5,618.

Actually there is no requirement in law or reason for all instruction to take place at the college. Convenience might be better served in some cases if the college were extended to the locale of its students. Employers very often arrange time and facilities for personnel who wish to take course work. Another possible advantage to this approach is that those who feel ill at ease in the formal college setting or who have some anxiety about the inevitable institutional earmarks of education and educators may be more inclined to consider study possibilities in an environment familiar to them.

Offering Community Services

Beyond the regularly scheduled classes of the college, whether held by day or by night or whatever the place in the district, the community college offers other important educational, cultural, and recreational benefits to the community. Naturally enough, these are called community services. One authority suggests that the college has two sets of responsibilities in this regard:

As a catalyst in community development and self-improvement. The college provides leadership, coordination, and cooperation to stimulate action programs.

As a locus for the cultural, intellectual, and social development of its district community.[2]

The range of these services is broad. They seem limited only by the creativity of leadership, the objectives of the institution, interest in the community, the means available, and provisions made by other institutions and organizations. Commonly included are educational workshops, seminars, institutes, and special lectures; community research and development; widespread use of college facilities by community groups; varied cultural programs; community guidance and counseling; cooperation with employers and placement agencies; the utilization of the physical and human resources of the community in the instructional program of the college; public information; and many others.

More than a hundred cultural organizations perform annually on the campus of a California community college. Cultural events range from an annual series of concerts by a leading symphony orchestra to youth symphony concerts, opera, ballet and modern dance, chamber music, drama, vocal concerts for children, and art exhibits. All of these are in addition to the college-sponsored series of cultural events, art films, and exhibits.

Another college has developed an outstanding recreation program for its area attracting more than 30,000 participants in the summer. Besides the usual physical activities such as swimming, team sports, gymnastics, league play, and track and field, the program features work in art, music, and drama.

Summer music camps for junior high and high school students, art workshops, and theaters for children are other ongoing programs of community service. Thus all ages and occupations are provided for, including elementary and high school students. Use of library facilities, planetarium programs, exhibits, and educational radio and television is extended to all.

Although community services are specified increasingly in state educational plans as a community college function, California has a decided advantage over many other states. Under the Community Services Act of 1951, California junior college districts are permitted to exceed their legal tax maximum figure by five cents on each $100 of assessed valuation. This provision gives them an unusual opportunity to provide broad programs of community services.

Now a field of new and major importance faces the community college, calling for an expansion of services much beyond their present scope and focused upon the needs of out-of-school youth and adults who live in the inner cities of the nation's metropolitan areas. Two recent developments account in part for the stepped-up interest which is readily apparent. The first is the experience of some community colleges with various antipoverty programs, including "Upward Bound." (Under federal funds special summer programs are established for high school students who are considered to have college potential but who, for economic, cultural, or other reasons, might not continue their education.) The second — much more compelling — is the very fact of the existence of these institutions in many cities where they were unknown just a few years ago. Their appearance in highly urban settings makes inescapable a concern about their social and physical environments.

Since 1960 community colleges have been established for the first time in these cities:

Philadelphia	Seattle
Boston	Portland
Pittsburgh	Spokane
Cleveland	Birmingham
St. Louis	Dayton
Miami	Minneapolis
Dallas	Newark
Fort Worth	Rochester

They have served other major cities, such as Los Angeles, San Francisco, New York, and Chicago, for much longer periods. Many are in the first year or two of their operation. So at the same time that this nation seeks almost desperately to make its cities livable, the community college emerges as a potentially valuable resource to be used in that effort.

Campus Location

One of the first perplexing questions to be answered by the planners of an urban college is where to locate the campus. This question is inevitably related to another: whom should the institution serve? Shall the campus or campuses be in the suburbs or downtown or somewhere in between? Values other than educational come into the picture. Can the college be used to advantage in urban renewal programs or to revitalize the downtown section? These and additional important considerations are weighed as the issue of accessibility is decided. Most metropolitan areas provide multiple units of the college so that the entire population finds the services within reach. However, it is clear that making educational opportunity obtainable means more strenuous effort and different approaches in some areas of the city from those required in others. The inner city, with its disadvantages in unemployment, substandard housing, illiteracy, school dropouts, and minority group membership, demands particular attention.

Youths who are not in school and adults living below the poverty line constitute a large portion of the inner city population. Theoretically, the deprived family in the inner city has just as much right and just as much opportunity for community college education as do middle-class citizens in the suburbs. The unemployed adult over 30 years of age can enjoy the same community college advantages as the youth who graduates from high school. And opportunity for specific job training is just as available to the disadvantaged youth as it is to the student from a more comfortable situation. But the poor in the inner city have in part created their own barriers, partly psychological and partly due to lack of understanding, to taking advantage of the community colleges' open doors. And the colleges in the past have ignored and neglected these people, failing to reach out to them and to destroy the barriers. Today, ways are being found to involve the poor in programs at the community college level which will help them help themselves to find social fulfillment.

Inner-City Challenges

Harold Gores, president of the Educational Facilities Laboratories, recently called upon the community college to face up to the responsibilities indicated by these conditions:

> Education, and particularly the community college, may be the best hope of the inner city. The battle ground is in the city — stay and fight where you are. Don't turn your back and run to the suburbs. The community college may be the only acceptable agency for saving the central city. Maybe you have to be put into the neighborhood business. The people trust you. They depend on you.[3]

The need is so evident that few question the placement of some college facilities in or adjacent to the inner city. But there is much intense debate about the kinds of educational services the institution should provide. An increasing sense of commitment to doing something is quite apparent. What to do and how to do it pose a quandary. Representatives of a dozen big-city community colleges said as much a short time ago:

> Needless to say, we are not yet doing the job that needs to be done in the inner city. There have been disappointments, false starts, experiments that have fallen short of their goals. This was inevitable considering the task at hand. To be an instrument of social change the community college must take on a new dimension in planning its programs and its physical facilities.

It must invade the educational vacuums where help is needed. It must reach out with expert, probing fingers and pull in students to get to the crucial source of social ills, and educational voids.

Admittedly this is not easy, nor is it the exclusive obligation of the community college. But, working with other agencies of the city, county, state, and federal government as well as other existing institutions, we must offer services on the spot, where they are needed . . . and more of the atmosphere that stimulates hope and inspiration.[4]

Big-city community colleges, some of very recent founding, are compelled to deal with circumstances which, although not new in themselves, possess a new moral force and urgency. A productive educational response is required. But there are no answers in the back of the book; in former periods the population of the inner city was of concern to the college community only as an object of research.

How does the college proceed? In a number of cities program development is being guided by these assumptions: that adults — the poor, the unemployed, the undereducated — should have educational opportunity provided in an adult setting, in a broad context of learning which encourages open-ended educational and occupational mobility; that poor adults need job training and jobs, but that they have equally important needs for knowledge and skills to play their roles as parents, consumers, citizens, and continuing learners; that the poor need to be involved in planning, operating, and evaluating the programs and services which the colleges will provide and, furthermore, that they require training to fill these roles effectively. The community college, with its local base and orientation, has advantages which qualify it as an appropriate vehicle for these new programs.

Obviously, some adaptation of conventional measures — some experimentation — is in order. Some possibilities are new types of associate degree curriculums; new programs below the two-year degree level and/or less than two years in length for literacy or skill improvement, self-development, occupational skill attainment and improvement, general education, and other educational goals; changed concepts of enrollment patterns and work-study programs; better opportunities for educational and occupational mobility for those who are rejected by the collegiate establishment; student personnel and other services tailored to the needs of the inner-city students; job development, and a wide range of community services.

A new sense of community identity, participation and involvement is the aim of a program of "outreach" into the inner city of Oakland, California, by the Peralta Colleges. A Student Service Corps will carry on a work-study service program of community outreach, development, and service in the inner city. One hundred fifty students are being paid to work in community organizations and public agencies in the inner city. Community Development Centers are providing educational and counseling services. The centers are also serving as the focal points for workshops and other programs initiated under a community enrichment program. They will also facilitate the supervision and administration of the Student Service Corps. The Enrichment Program is to provide workshops in art, music, and drama, to be supplemented by recreational, social, cultural, and educational experience at the block, neighborhood, and community level. A Scholarship-Subsistence Project is designed to provide financial assistance to residents of the inner city who wish to attend college to prepare themselves for careers in public service. Spokesmen for the college district maintain that by taking the educational, cultural, and human resources of the colleges into the community in this fashion, the district can demonstrate not only how the community college can serve the inner city but how residents of the inner city can be involved as active participants in the task of serving their neighbors.

Chicago City College has initiated a neighborhood project for adults who are parents of disadvantaged students in the community college. The program focuses on better literacy training, preparation for the General Educational Development examinations (for the high school certificate), job counseling and placement, and other related educational services. Community education and employments aides are not only trained by the college but are also employed by the institution to work with adults in need of educational-employment services under the supervision of professionals. A community council was asked to plan the project and sponsor its activities.

In Los Angeles and Cleveland, the counseling function is highlighted. In the Los Angeles community college program, disadvantaged second-year students are trained and then employed as part-time counselor-aides to assist new students with similar poverty backgrounds. They are expected to provide a degree and quality of psychological support to the new students which professional counselors are unable to give because of the socio-educational gap that exists between them and the students, and the lack of immediacy of assistance they are prepared to give. The community college in Cleveland has established a neighborhood counseling center in the inner city where residents can obtain information and assistance in finding new educational opportunities at the college and elsewhere, and in taking advantage of these opportunities.

Experimentation is under way in a number of other cities as well to determine more effective ways of reaching all persons who can benefit from college programs. Many students will not show up at the college without an intermediary contact. They have a stereotyped image of the institution in which selectivity, competition, money requirements, the establishment, books, and administrators and faculty who live in another world loom large. Communication cannot be brought about with them by making field trips into the places where they live. The college has to be there substantially enough to belong. The Borough of Manhattan Community College acknowledged this in a series of seminars with architects and community leaders which preceded the planning of new facilities. "Who are the ought-to-be students and how do we reach them through program and facilities?" was the dominant question.

Among the means of communication suggested, the creation of counseling services and community centers throughout the area which the college wishes to serve, and the involvement of indigenous personnel show most promise. The employment as advisory aides of those who have already taken advantage of the college opportunities has also been a productive measure, not only in terms of attracting the students initially but in maintenance of informed liaison between the professional staff and the often dubious first-time student. These and other efforts of this kind are based upon the notion that educational opportunity does not really exist for those who are unaware of it.

Another prominent element in these experimental and demonstration programs is the conviction that the college must not seek to become an island or fortress cut off from its surroundings. In a variety of ways recognition is given of the social environment in which the college exists.

Because of its strategic setting and its basic aim of extending educational opportunity, the community college has leadership responsibilities in creative community development. It can serve as a center for analyzing local problems and for coordinating action programs. By the way it is designed the college can develop the leadership capacities of local citizens. As an institution the college is nonpartisan. All ethnic, religious, economic, and social interests and groups are represented in its clientele. The community, therefore, is provided with an instrumentality for examining those problems which cut across all segments and are of common concern. A forum exists for constructive discussion and analysis of issues. Even beyond this, the community college is under some obligation to cultivate in those who use its services the skills of argument and deliberation. Moreover, the resources of competence of the college staff are available as these are sought and as they are relevant to problems under consideration. No institution today has greater potential as an integrative influence than the community college.

Self-Effort

There are other characteristics of the community college which have strong bearing on one of the most important elements in individual and community development, that of self-effort. Education means, or ought to mean, learning, and learning requires self-effort. No institution can learn for anyone. It is essential, therefore, that the work of the college be joined to efforts in housing, public health, and similar programs. Housing or health programs or other measures designed to change environmental factors do not necessarily change people. On the other hand, the college has as its major aim stimulation of learning effort, so that each person with whom it is in contact becomes capable not only of reacting sensibly to his environment but of dealing with it, helping to shape it.

Self-effort in its corporate expression comes close to what social scientists have agreed must have priority in dealing with frustrations in the big cities: local control of neighborhood institutions. They have seen it work on a small scale and they think it will work more widely. The idea of local control is not a new one for community colleges. In most states the governing boards are elected from citizens served by the institution. Typically there are dozens of active advisory committees for all kinds of college programs. Community leadership is not only identified through the work of these groups but developed through responsible action. Thus the model of locally oriented and locally controlled institutions already exists. Now it shows promise as an organization not only to achieve educational ends but in that very process to effectuate community improvement. However, there is a definite trend toward larger districts and greater state-level control. The presumed advantages in bigger organizational structures must be weighed carefully against the value of significant local involvement.

Widened Responsibilities

How to achieve effective district organization is just one of many problems to confront the community college as it steps up its activities in continuing education and community services. Apparent immediately is the question raised by both those within and those outside of community college ranks. Are such activities really the business of a community college? During the discussions which preceded passage of the Higher Education Act of 1965 with its Title I for community services, congressional committees and educational circles made repeated reference to *university* extension. Community college spokesmen sought clarification of the language which would assure inclusion of their institutions for these services. University and government personnel were not resistant; they favored community college participation. However, they had difficulty seeing the community college in a role which seemed much more familiar in the university context. That these services might be a major function of the community college appeared more a matter of conjecture than of fact, and such a view was justified because it is the potential rather than performance to date which carries the greater import.

Not until 1967 was a community college accepted for membership in the National University Extension Association, an organization founded in 1915 whose member universities and colleges have an interest in continuing education and public service. Also in 1967, for the first time four community colleges were granted membership in the Association of University Evening Colleges. This organization is made up of 150 institutions in the United States and Canada with programs in "collegiate evening education."

Although continuing education has been a function of community colleges for many years, community service as a field is not so well developed. Reputable authorities, while recognizing it as a part of the college program, along with transfer and vocational-technical education, judge that performance in this area leaves a good deal to be desired. In part this inadequacy is attributable to a scale of institutional values which, in former years at least, placed transfer programs first, occupational education second, and community services a somewhat distant third. There is substantial evidence that the relative positions are changing, in accordance with societal demands. Other deterrents to more rapid development exist, however.

One of them has to do with money. The first operations threatened when the financial situation gets tight are those concerned with continuing education and community services. They are apparently considered frills by some administrators, board members, and legislators and therefore easily to be dispensed with. The concept of a society in which opportunity for continuous learning is not optional but essential will need repeated explanation.

Another problem which has delayed fuller expression of community services is the all-consuming task of starting a college — and more often than not in an unbelievably short time. Necessarily concentration of effort has been upon programs that the community perceives to mean "college." Very probably the taxpayers were sold on the merits of the institution as a stepping stone to employment or transfer to a four-year college. Community services and continuing education are lower on the list of priorities. But with the early years of organization behind them — with the well-known collegiate offerings established — the large number of community colleges founded during the last few years are achieving, with the support of their communities, greater breadth of services.

In this field, as in occupational education, the community college joins other institutions already at work. Public schools have been at the job of adult education for a long time. Universities have a distinguished history in community service and educational extension. Clearly, a division of labor is needed. There is too often little or no cooperative planning or coordination at either the local or the state level. Even educational institutions long in the field are not certain of the services best undertaken by other groups, nor are they clear on their own role in the total instructional effort or at the community coordinating table. Some improvement has resulted from the requirement in the Higher Education Act of 1965 for a state plan of community services, but the difficult problem of identifying appropriate roles for the various kinds of institutions remains unresolved. A reasonable delineation of the job to be done by each institution was proposed by a seminar of experts in the field meeting at the University of Michigan.[5] In looking at their own state and attempting to reduce duplication and omission of programs and unnecessary competition for financial support, clientele, facilities, and personnel, the seminar participants recommended these tentative instructional roles and coordinating functions at the local level:

1. *The Public Schools* should take the leadership role in initiating a local advisory and coordinating council made up of all educational groups and interested adults in the community. This function belongs, most logically, in the public school because it is publicly supported, concerned with broad educational problems, has facilities located throughout the community and has a membership which includes all segments of the population. Most successful curriculum areas are Americanization, elementary and high school completion, business and distribution, practical arts and crafts, homemaking and family living.

2. *The Community College,* where one exists, should supplement the ongoing local community program, particularly in the areas of formal transfer of credit, technical-terminal classes, creative arts, and cultural enrichment.

3. *The Community College* may also serve as a coordinating agent for local programs on a regional basis. The regional agent would provide a "meeting-house" where cooperative planning could eliminate program duplication and competition. Local communities that are unable to provide their own resources to meet a particular need could draw on the resources of the regional agent.

4. *Universities and Four-year Colleges,* where available, should provide local communities with extension credit and enrichment non-credit classes, such as cultural and personnel improvement, civic and community affairs. However, the main functions of the higher institutions of learning should be research, consultant service to local programs through workshops and conferences, and degree programs for adult education teachers and administrators.

5. Where an active adult education program is provided by neither the local public schools nor a community college, the university should serve as the coordinating agency to assist local institutions to initiate and operate an adult program.

Similar guidelines have been adopted as policy in the State of Florida. In effect, they specify that each institution should be encouraged to offer the services which are most in harmony with its primary mission and which it is most competent to supply. Cooperative and coordinative arrangements are sought. It could well be a responsibility of the community college, because of its strategic location and the size of its district, to ascertain whether community educational needs are in fact being met and to insure that a program of services is initiated to meet them by local institutions.

A great deal of discussion currently is under way about the necessity for "urban extension." Unquestionably, patterns of educational services which were devised to suit the practical requirements of a rural population must find an equivalent expression today in an urban culture. Proposals have been made for urban-grant universities in some sixty-seven cities.[6] These would take their places alongside the sixty-seven land-grant universities established under the Morrill Act of 1862 "for the benefit of agriculture and mechanic arts . . . without excluding other scientific and classical studies . . . in order to promote the liberal and practical education of the industrial classes."[7] Now it is envisioned that urban universities would "share responsibility not only for all levels of education and health, but for equality of opportunity as well."

There is surely little question about the need for such institutions. However, as states plan for these essential services, a new fact must be taken into account: the existence of the community college with its broad charter of services in almost every major city. The attributes of the community college are in line with many of the critical educational needs of our urban environment. Society has an educational instrument, nonexistent when land-grant universities were authorized or when university extension services were initiated, available to play a significant part in a total program of education in the cities of the nation. As new institutions are founded, sound public policy would suggest that in their appropriate role they be utilized *in concert with* the community college in its appropriate role.

The community college has special responsibilities because of its orientation and proximity to the people. It is guided by the notion that is should provide a variety of educational experiences to meet a variety of needs, interests, and abilities, and that these experiences should be available at low cost to anyone who can benefit from them. Undoubtedly, where this institution is at its best it reaches out to the people who comprise its environment, involves them, identifies with them, is of them and by them.

NOTES

[1] Annual Report of the President, Miami-Dade Junior College, Miami, Fla., 1966.

[2] Ervin L. Harlacher, "California's Community Renaissance," *Junior College Journal*, April 1964.

[3] Bud Weidenthal, *The Community College Commitment to the Inner City*. Washington: American Association of Junior Colleges, 1967.

[4] *Ibid.*

[5] Gale Jensen, "Problems Restricting the Development of Continuing and Adult Education in the State of Michigan." University of Michigan Adult Directors Seminar, Dearborn, August 12, 1966.

[6] Fred M. Hechinger, "A Call for the 'Urban-Grant' College," *New York Times*, October 22, 1967.

[7] *Ibid.*

6

STAFF—THE
DECISIVE FACTOR

BERGEN COMMUNITY COLLEGE IN NEW JERSEY —
a new college interviewing candidates for Fall 1968
opening — top salaries — fringe benefits — positions
available for chairmen of the following departments —
Business — Health and physical education, Humanities
and Social Science — Nursing, Science and
Mathematics. Full and part-time day and/or evening
faculty in areas listed above. Master's degree required.

NEW COMMUNITY COLLEGE — in historic Morris
County, New Jersey. For September 1968 opening seek
faculty applicants for full and part-time day and evening
positions in Humanities, Social Sciences, Biological
Sciences, Physical Sciences, Nursing, Business,
Secretarial, Data Processing, Police Administration,
Mathematics, Graphics, Electrical/Electronics, and
Mechanical Technologies. Excellent salaries and fringe
benefits. Prefer Master's in subject. Industry, science
and/or teaching experience desirable.

— *New York Times*
October 22, 1967

More than fifty community colleges will join those in Bergen and Morris counties, New Jersey, in opening to students for the first time in September, 1968. On the average each will want 100 faculty and administrative staff members to meet the 1,000 to 1,500 students it will enroll. And these institutions will find that more than six hundred counterparts in most of the states are seeking to accommodate mounting enrollments and to replace persons who have retired or gone to other positions. Reasonable estimates place the need for new professional personnel in community colleges at more than 10,000 each year. In a society eagerly searching for talent in almost every field, it is no wonder that one of the first questions asked by those who are curious about the merits of the community college is, Where will you get the teachers and administrators; how will you staff these institutions? Although not so apparent, a more significant question is whether additions to the working force of an institution with new and multiple educational assignments, whatever the number needed, can be qualified to facilitate the attainment of its distinctive goals.

The series of institutional decisions which put Mr. Smith at the teacher's desk in the classroom and Mr. Jones in the president's office has its beginning with the board of directors of the college. Elected or appointed, the board is the legal entity held accountable for the institution by the community or the state. Characteristically, board members are not professional educators. Their occupational backgrounds are diversified. In most states now they have responsibility for only the community college. The board's tasks require its members to have a keen sense of judgment, a knowledge of the community, and the capacity to assume the legal and financial accountability specified under the statutes which brought the institution into being,

During the present period of rapid expansion in the community college field, many boards find themselves to be newly organized institutional bodies but without administrative personnel, faculty, facilities, or program. Their immediate duty is to take steps which will result in opening doors to students within the shortest possible time.

Selecting a President

In almost all cases the board begins by looking for a president. This can be done in various ways. Some boards advertise in newspapers and journals. Others bring in a consultant from a university or another organization to assist them in thinking through the process of locating candidates and establishing procedures by which an appropriate selection can be made. However, before the board selects its president it faces the difficult but essential task of determining, if only in tentative form, what kind of college it wants. Where does the board look for help in this process?

Guidelines may exist in the state laws which authorized the institution. Where there is a state-level agency for community colleges, counsel and literature are available. Yet boards often operate in a framework which allows a good deal of leeway. Although basic and minimum requirements and standards may be prescribed, they can and will determine the character of the institution through their selection of leadership personnel and the policies they make, support, and interpret to the community. The way a president is chosen is consequently of great importance not only because a wise selection is essential but because the selection can be wise only to the extent that the board sharpens its view of the job to be done by the institution. How can the decision be made as to whether Mr. A or Mr. B will be the better choice unless each candidate with his respective attributes is matched against some concept of what the college will be? So, by the questions it asks and by what it looks for in candidates the board of directors is in effect sketching in broad strokes (and sometimes in painful detail) its conception of the shape of the new institution.

Accordingly, the choosing of a president gives a board, old or new, an unparalleled opportunity to consider the basic aims of the institution. The very process of intelligent interviewing becomes something of a seminar for board and candidate as they test the validity of their ideas.

What does a board look for? What qualities are important? Is a school superintendency a desirable background? Or a university professorship? Should the president hold a doctorate? How would a top businessman do in the position? Or a retired military officer? Such questions are not entirely without significance, but a board might better begin conversations that would reveal the candidate's attitudes and abilities as measured against the following criteria:

Conviction of the worth and dignity of each individual for what he is and what he can become. Commitment to the idea that society ought to provide the opportunity for each person to continue appropriate education up to the limit of his potential.

Appreciation of the social worth of a wide range of aptitudes, talents, interests, and types of intelligence. Respect for translating these into suitable educational programs.

Understanding of the interpersonal processes by which the individual comes to be what he is. Appreciation for the interaction of the college and other social institutions and agencies — the community, family, and church organizations — in providing a social milieu for personality development.

Knowledge of community structure and processes. Capacity to identify structures of social power and the decision makers involved in various kinds of community issues.

Understanding of education in our society and viewpoints about its role. Acquaintance with critical contemporary issues in education. Appreciation of the responsibilities of elementary and secondary education as well as those of higher education.

Commitment to community college services as part of a total educational program. Constructive and affirmative views toward the assignment of the comprehensive open-door institution.

Some understanding of the elements at work which are changing society throughout the world. Awareness of the significance of population growth, shifts in population, changes in age composition of population, the dynamics of aspirations and ambitions in cultures on all continents, the rapidity of technological development, societal resistance to self-examination and criticism, and other developments foretelling social change.

Ability to listen, understand, interpret, and reconcile. Capacity to communicate.

Board members will probably have in mind three other questions as they size up a candidate: Has this man enough stature in the field of education so that the leadership of other educational institutions will have respect for him and hence for this new institution we are creating? Or if not now, does he have potential in this regard? Do his attainments suggest to the community that the institution holds marked promise because it can attract a man of this caliber? And most important, What is there about him to persuade outstanding people to join in making this a superior institution?

Whether or not he possesses the Ph.D. or its equivalent is not the main consideration. If he does have it and still meets the basic criteria of interests, attitudes, and understandings, as well as that ingredient which commends him to his educational peers, the community, and his future colleagues, well and good. He should be hired.

Interpreting the Community College to the Community

The Board's job is not finished when the president has been signed up. The welfare of the college cannot be fully delegated to other hands, no matter how capable. A demanding and continuing obligation of the board is to insure that the institution is free to fulfill its mission, and part of this obligation is interpreting the college as a place for learning to the community. People learn (find out, discover, gain knowledge, understanding, and skills) by study and instruction and investigation. Board members need to form a concept of what learning means in terms of their policies, because without doubt they will be called upon by various community interests to justify discussions, activities, and behavior of students or faculty or administrative personnel which some will consider improper or unsuitable. Prompt and serious repercussions from problems of this kind are the inevitable result of local control and local orientation, however valuable the latter are. No space or time cushion exists between the members of the board and their constituents. An immediate accounting is called for by people within driving distance or quick telephone contact.

Examples of issues which will confront the board are current and numerous. In Chicago a complaint was made that a book used in an evening class in contemporary literature was unsuitable as required reading and should be withdrawn. Spirited debate ensued in the press. The board was required to make its judgments in the spotlight of local and national publicity — What shall college students read? Who shall choose their reading matter? What should be the roles of the administration and the board of trustees in such an issue? After reviewing actions taken by the administrative personnel of the college, the board concurred in the view that the curriculum of an institution of higher education is developed by the faculty, within a general policy framework established by the board of trustees, and that the faculty has the right and the responsibility to develop courses and select materials of instruction which are necessary to the course objectives. Further, the board decided that the right of the faculty to develop appropriate courses and materials carries with it the responsibility to insure relevance to what is being taught, and the way in which it is being taught. The administration of the college has the obligation to select a well-prepared, responsible staff and then to stimulate and support them in the development of the program of education in the college.

"Should your tax money be used to support communist speakers on campus?" was the caption of an advertisement in a California newspaper attacking the College of San Mateo for permitting the chairman of the Communist Party of Northern California to speak on campus. A crowd of some 300 persons gathered for a three-hour board meeting during which speakers vigorously debated the controversial invitation to an avowed communist to appear as one of a series of speakers in the student body's cultural series program. The trustees were urged by one group to block the appearance of the Communist "agent" and to adopt a resolution of permanent policy prohibiting known Communists from speaking on a "tax supported platform." The president of the college, in defending the students' invitation, stated that, "It is the college policy to hear all sides of all issues."

Guided by a "controversial issues policy" previously developed by faculty-student committees and adopted as school policy, the board remained firm in its decision to allow the speaker to appear before the student body. The 1967 statement is an excellent example of the way a community college board meets its obligation to create a framework of principles within which the objectives of the college can be effectively met:

Study of Controversial Issues[1]

a. Assumptions Basic to District Policy

    (1) That free discussion is a right extended to thoughtful citizens, but that no one has the right to abuse this freedom by advocating the overthrow of the government by force.

    (2) That a free society functions efficiently only if its citizens have the right to discuss, to debate, and to disagree constructively.

(3) That the Constitutional guarantee of freedom of speech is meaningful only to the extent that the majority is willing to hear honest expressions of unpopular ideas by minority groups.

(4) That an educated citizenry, fully aware of all the evidence, is best able to preserve the valuable heritage of American democratic institutions.

(5) That College of San Mateo has an obligation to its community to promote healthy discussion as an educative force.

(6) That our way of life is attractive enough and our institutions are sturdy enough to stand comparison with any which exist in any culture.

(7) That the truth will prevail in the market place of ideas.

b. District Policy

(1) Within the framework of the orderly processes of our democratic Constitutional society, the faculty of College of San Mateo will have freedom to consider all issues which will contribute to the development of its students. The criteria to be followed in selecting issues for study will be:

(a) The issue should contribute to the prescribed course of study and the general education program of the College.

(b) It should be of sufficient interest to encourage participation by the students.

(c) It should provide opportunity for critical thinking, tolerance and understanding of conflicting points of view.

(d) It should be one about which sufficient information is available to allow for discussion and evaluation on a factual and reasonable basis.

(2) Pursuant to this adopted policy, the administration, the available faculty, or student organizations may sponsor speakers of any shade of opinion.

(a) Approval of campus speakers is a function of the Superintendent.

(b) Speakers will be governed by the regulations of the College as to time, place and manner of public presentations.

(c) The Superintendent will encourage the presentation of the widest possible range of points of view.

No college can operate without toes being stepped on. No college can determine the reaction of its students or faculty to vital — or even trivial — issues. The cultivation of an environment of responsible inquiry and intellectual curiosity is bound to produce its critics as well as bestow its benefits. And this situation leads to a major question: Can an environment for learning be safeguarded in an educational institution whose policy makers are subject to possible social, economic, or political pressures from factions and individuals in their districts? An affirmative answer needs to be written into the policies which guide the institution, and interpreted continuously to its constituents. Such action by the board is the model for all other leadership within that institution.

The Job of Administration

What has the board to offer its prospective president? What is he to do? He will find his assignment demanding and complex, particularly in an urban institution with its swelling enrollments and urgent environmental problems. The president must lead in the interpretation of the character of the comprehensive community institution, especially if it is new. He must see to it that the board, administration, faculty, students, and community have a working understanding of what the role of the college is. Say the word "college" and all parties within hearing will have a picture in their minds, but the odds are that the pictures will be more different than alike. This is not to say that the president's view is the only acceptable one or that it ought to be dominant, but it is the president's business to encourage the process by which a college "self-concept" can emerge. Obviously decisions requiring judgments of suitability, relevance, or appropriateness of programs, policies, or procedures cannot be made rationally if such a self-concept is lacking. But this is a moving picture. The institution is in process of creating its identity. Leadership will sensitize the signal-receiving apparatus of the college so that the educational response is to add, delete, or adapt.

Not only are the community and the college constantly changing; so are concepts of administration. All that remains of the patriarchal president who spoke benevolently of "my faculty" is a slightly nostalgic memory. Now everybody "wants in on the act." Faculty and students want to be involved where their interests are at stake. And those interests have wide applicability to the college program and procedure. Both a form of organization and a point of view are called for which result in an accommodation of all who participate in the learning process through division of labor related to their professional preparation and institutional assignments. New forms of organization may very well be needed. Whether the patterns of organization commonly used in business, industry, labor, or the universities are entirely appropriate to the community college is manifestly open to question. The president of today's changing community college will need to marshal the ingenuity and intelligence of the people who comprise the institution in order to comprehend its tasks and formulate an organization both efficient and effective. He must initiate the interaction of professionals with mutual appreciation of roles and responsibilities.

The president will need also to be knowledgeable and persuasive in maintaining equilibrium in an institution widely diversified in fields of study and levels within those fields. He is involved with several thousand students each year. He must find the necessary numbers of new faculty, remodel old buildings, acquire new sites, build whole campuses. Since all this has to be done against fantastic deadlines, the problem of communication is compounded and the time for contemplation seldom found. Furthermore, the means by which the college does its work must be sought in a societal context increasingly competitive with other social demands.

Where does the board look for candidates — volunteers or draftees — for this important post? Today's presidents have backgrounds different from those of a generation or even a decade ago. Formerly secondary administration or the school superintendency seemed to be part of a career line to the community college presidency. Now a large proportion of the new presidents come from within the community college field. Miami, Dallas, Fort Worth, Cleveland, St. Louis, Dayton, and Oakland are among the cities which persuaded men already holding community college presidencies that building a new institution was an opportunity they could not reject. However, other new big-city institutions have chosen from other sources; a university dean of students who also served as chairman of the state board for community colleges, a dean of an old and respected institute of technology, and an officer of a nationally known consulting firm which had community colleges among its clients have become presidents. Dozens of institutions are headed by persons who were formerly vice-presidents or campus directors in other community college districts.

The Preparation of Administrators

The first concerted and systematic approach to the preparation of professional leadership was begun in 1960 by ten universities, the W. K. Kellogg Foundation, and the American Association of Junior Colleges. The universities, almost all still with an active interest, were

University of California at Los Angeles	University of Texas
University of California at Berkeley	Columbia University
Stanford University	Wayne State University
University of Michigan	University of Florida
Michigan State University	Florida State University

With the help of scholarship funds provided by the foundation, the universities launched a vigorous program to recruit potential administrators. The Junior College Leadership Program, as it came to be known, ordinarily began with the master's degree as a prerequisite and called for two years of study and internship leading to the doctorate. Every effort was made by the universities to keep their programs realistic in terms of field conditions. Leading community college practitioners came to the campuses frequently as consultants and resource personnel and to arrange for candidates to intern in their institutions. The American Association of Junior Colleges published announcements and brochures describing the program which were distributed to all graduate schools, to community colleges, and to individuals who expressed an interest in the career possibilities. As a result of the Junior College Leadership Program scores of administrative personnel have advanced to responsible positions during the past seven years. Usually they do not move directly into the position of president. The program was devised to prepare not only presidents but highly qualified personnel for a variety of administrative responsibilities. However, with a few years of experience added to their university training, these administrators quickly attract the attention of boards searching for chief executive officers.

In the process of developing programs for administrative personnel, the universities became valuable resource centers for information and research covering almost all aspects of community college operations. Both formal and informal placement activities increased. Boards looking for presidents tended to make early contact with the university centers, hoping to get the names of former participants in the program who had the qualifications and could be persuaded to leave their present positions.

The Junior College Leadership Program accounted in large part for a greatly stepped-up pace in research. In the period 1918–1963, 608 dissertations which had relevance to the junior college were reported nationally. On the other hand, 214 were completed in just three years, 1964–1966.

Although the preparation programs were initiated with substantial foundation support, now almost all the cooperating universities have agreed to indefinite continuance and other universities have recently added similar programs. The importance of these actions is clearly evident in the growing supply of qualified administrators and beyond that in the identification of community college administration as a career objective.

The Faculty

Nothing of such scale and coherence has been done to prepare community college teachers. Yet the annual need for new faculty, by the most reasonable estimates, is more than 10,000. The federal government has provided funds for the preparation of elementary and secondary school teachers, on the one hand, and graduate fellowship programs leading to the doctorate on the other. Neither provision fits the pattern of preparation most commonly required for community college faculty personnel. This is also the case with regard to foundation-supported efforts. Large sums have been spent to better prepare elementary and secondary teachers, and although impressive steps have been taken to attract and qualify college teachers, the effect of the latter program was to move candidates along to the doctorate as well as to a university career. The university undoubtedly benefited, but few if any of the people trained by this route joined community college teacher ranks.

No large-scale deliberate and concentrated program of development is yet in existence for prospective or currently employed community college teachers. However, a large number of universities and state colleges, aware of the need, are evidencing an interest which ranges from tentative to substantial. Many of them are ready to do a great deal more, but they acknowledge troublesome questions that must be dealt with before they can proceed very far or fast. Where are the teachers coming from now? Is community college teaching to be regarded as a career field? Can it be that attractive? How does preparation of the community college teacher differ from that of the secondary school teacher or the four-year college teacher?

The easiest questions to answer deal with the sources of teachers. Reports from Florida show that in 1964–1965, of every hundred new community college teachers, thirty-six came from the graduate schools of the universities, fourteen from college and university teaching, twenty-seven from high school teaching, and ten from a business occupation. The remainder were from miscellaneous sources. After six years of operation Miami-Dade Junior College, one of the largest in the country, prepared a faculty profile. Of the 477 members of the full-time instructional staff in 1965–1966, 28 per cent were from other colleges and universities, 23.4 per cent from private business and industry, 31 per cent from public school systems, and 11.5 per cent directly from graduate schools. The rest were from varied sources.

A national study of teacher supply and demand reports that 30 per cent of the new junior college teachers came directly from high school classrooms, 17 per cent from college and university teaching, 24 per cent from graduate schools, and 11.3 per cent from business occupations.[2]

Further information comes from a California study. In that state most community college teachers have never attended a community college; 63 per cent of the new full-time teachers reported in 1963 that they had never been students in the kind of institution in which they were teaching. Further, 60 per cent of them decided to enter teaching after reaching twenty-one years of age; 71 per cent described the occupational background of their father as "semi-professional, sales-clerical, skilled or unskilled"; 55 per cent had taught previously for five or more years; 53 per cent said they prefer to continue teaching in a community college; and 27 per cent would like to move into teaching in a four-year college or university.[3]

There is evidence nationally that the public schools provide a decreasing percentage of the new teachers in community colleges whereas the number coming directly from graduate school programs is rising. This trend has caused some concern, for reasons that are referred to by the staff of the coordinating council in California. "Intensive experience with teachers of this caliber suggests that they are making and will make a significant contribution to junior college education. Nevertheless, their interests are frequently devoted more to teaching transfer students of high ability than to teaching the more typical junior college student." The council's report emphasized that it would be necessary "for colleges to give more importance to in-service training of new teachers."[4]

National studies over an eight-year period (1957–1965) show no significant change in the proportion of *new* junior college teachers who hold the doctorate (6.2 per cent in 1964–1965) or those with one year of advanced credit beyond the master's degree (20.7 per cent). The proportion of new teachers holding the master's degree rose from 43.6 per cent to 51.3 per cent while that of new teachers starting full-time service before achieving a master's degree declined from 28.1 per cent to 21.8 per cent.[5] Incidentally, about 9 per cent of all junior and community college teachers hold the doctorate. Some will complete the work for their doctor's degree after they enter their teaching field.

The Problem of Credentials

Not only is a decreasing proportion of new teachers for community colleges coming from the public schools, but certification or credentials requirements, which have their basis in the public school part of the community college heritage, are undergoing marked change. Formerly certain patterns of preparation were required if the teacher was in effect to be "licensed" for employment in a given state. Now the trend nationally is illustrated by action in California in 1966. The necessity for a junior college teacher to secure a teaching credential was eliminated by the state board of education. In general, a master's degree is sufficient evidence of professional preparation.

Mixed reactions have greeted the tendency toward credential discontinuance or liberalization. Although administrators were favorable toward less stringent requirements particularly with regard to courses in education, they wanted personnel with knowledge of the community college and with competence to teach the student body characteristic of this institution. However, with the credential requirement removed there was a decline in enrollment in university courses designed to prepare for community college teaching. Why? Two answers suggest themselves. First, when the motivating whip of the teaching credential was removed, the real reason for taking such certified courses also disappeared. And this situation prompts the second answer: that these programs may not be good enough to attract able candidates on their own merits. Regardless of whether these are valid answers, if some orientation to community college teaching tasks is desirable either the universities will have to demonstrate the value of the programs and make them attractive or the community colleges will have to assume much greater responsibility upon the induction of new personnel.

The Preparation of Community College Teachers

What kind of preparation is suitable for community college teachers? A number of moves are under way to find out. The Council of Graduate Schools in America and the American Council on Education have joined forces with the American Association of Junior Colleges to encourage universities to devote more thought to this problem. The same organizations have strongly urged an expansion of federal support of their efforts. Recently Duke University announced its Cooperative Program in Junior College Teaching. The University of Southern California has a Junior College Associate Teaching Program. The University of Tennessee, with Ford Foundation funds, offers a master of arts in college teaching after "a two-year enriched master's degree program for students who wish to teach in community, junior, and smaller four-year colleges." UCLA has a junior college teacher internship program. Some two hundred colleges and universities have reported that they do something toward preparation of community college teachers. How effective they are, of course, is the big question.

Actually, to generalize about the community college teacher's preparation is of limited use. The tasks within the comprehensive institution are extremely varied. There is a least common denominator — an understanding of the assignment of the comprehensive community college and sufficient acceptance of this concept to contribute purposefully and constructively toward its goals — and there are other common elements which relate to student characteristics. A broad distribution of academic aptitude and ability exists in the community college. Skillful teaching and counseling are called for by both the expectations and the needs of the students. Since many of the students are exploring fields of interests and are in the process of making more precise their educational and vocational objectives, they need to work with versatile professionals. The teacher will require not only breadth of knowledge but skill in "showing how" and in translating the abstract and symbolic into the practical and realistic. Those teachers responsible for the academic courses leading to university transfer will be required to have subject matter competence similar to that needed by teachers of lower-division courses in the university. And instructors in the remedial programs require university preparation which will equip them to deal with these kinds of problems. Typically, remedial instructors are not adequately prepared for the courses they are required to teach. They are learning about remedial students through an on-the-job process. The variety of patterns of preparation needed by community college faculty is further illustrated by requirements in the rapidly developing occupational fields. Here there is no adequate substitute for actual job experience.

How do the teachers themselves feel about their preparation? Recently, in a national study they were asked to sketch out their ideas of a sound program of preparation. The acceptable base would be the master's degree: the B.A. or B.S. plus thirty hours of credit, mainly in content (rather than in education or methods courses). But desirable preparation as described by many would include elements not now offered in M.A. programs. Adequately accomplished, these elements would require a postbaccalaureate period of study ranging from sixteen months to two years.

A minimum of ten courses (or the equivalent) is suggested in the subject discipline at the graduate level. Of these ten courses, half should be, to the extent possible, interdisciplinary in content and instruction. (Examples are biology-zoology-botany; sociology-psychology-anthropology; geography-geology-ecology.) At least one quarter, and preferably a full semester, of actual teaching in a cooperating community college, with at least two preparations, is also suggested. This is not conceived of as "practice teaching," in its traditional sense. Rather it is a bona fide internship, with supervision and counsel both from appropriate university faculty and from veteran junior college faculty in the discipline.

In place of separate course offerings in educational philosophy, educational psychology, and methods of teaching, teachers generally recommended what could be considered a continuing professional seminar, involving all graduate students, from whatever discipline, who were seeking this "enriched master's degree" for prospective teachers. The seminar would meet every other week through the entire span of the graduate program. It would have its own syllabus of appropriate reading material, including recognized works in the history of education, the nature of the learning process, the psychology (and problems) of students, the nature of teaching, and the like. Ideally, the seminar would be led by carefully trained teams of graduate professors and veteran community college instructors, or master teachers.

Such a program would be open ended. A successful completion would not hinder an interested student from going on for a doctorate if he wished. It could conceivably be completed in a summer-academic year-summer pattern, thus reducing the student's financial commitments. In most areas it would make him a desirable candidate for a community college faculty.[6]

There would be substantial agreement in the community college field that the program described is suitable for the teachers who carry responsibility for the academic courses which prepare the student for transfer. But for the occupational programs, different patterns of experience may be needed. The going becomes somewhat difficult at this point, though, because very little headway has been made in determining the best ways to qualify faculty for the occupational programs. One of the most promising developments is the Occupational Instructor Project at Southern Illinois University, a joint project of the Junior College District of St. Louis-St. Louis County and of SIU supported in part by a grant from the Ford Foundation. The program is designed to accommodate both those who plan to teach specialized occupational courses and those who will teach general education courses included in occupational curricula. It provides an opportunity to gain, before employment, an understanding of the philosophy, objectives, and organization of the community college and the post-secondary technical institute.

The program, which produced its first graduates in the spring of 1968, leads to the master's degree. About 15 per cent of the candidates' courses are in the community college and technical education fields, about 60 per cent in the subject areas which the student is preparing to teach, and 25 per cent in a one-semester teaching internship experience under the supervision of an experienced teacher in the St. Louis community college.

Eligible candidates are individuals who plan to teach students in the occupational programs of community colleges and who fulfill one of the following educational requirements: a bachelor's degree in an academic subject area commonly included in the general education portion of a curriculum for occupational students — e.g., English, mathematics, biological sciences, physical sciences, social sciences, or psychology; bachelor's degree in an occupational field appropriately related to agriculture, business, engineering and industrial technology, health or public service; two or more years of college-level work (but less than that required for a bachelor's degree) in an appropriate occupational curriculum.

The community-college internship program reaches out to those in business and industry who want to teach. Among the 1968 intern-teachers is a man with a background of seven years in a police department and a master's degree in criminology. He will teach law enforcement. A woman with seven years' experience as a nurse will teach nursing and public health. Her degree is a master of science in public health. A man with eighteen years of industrial experience and a master of science in research will teach electronics. A retired naval officer with twenty years of service experience and master's degrees in science and enginering from M.I.T. will teach mathematics and mechanical engineering. A substantial number of the sixteen interns in 1967–1968 had earned their masters' degrees in institutions other than Southern Illinois University. All of them participated in a one-semester full-time internship at one of the three colleges in the St. Louis Junior College District. This included working with experienced teachers in the intern's area of specialty and teaching a partial load. Observation of various teachers' classes, field assignments in industry, business or professional areas, and orientation sessions and seminars on the philosophy and organization of community college occupational programs rounded out their preparation.

Occupational Competence and Teaching

A comprehensive community college will employ many instructors who combine their occupational work in the professions or business or the trades with teaching. There is great potential benefit to the college program in their up-to-date knowledge of occupational field requirements and their own demonstrated occupational competence. However, for them, as for all of its faculty members, the college has an inescapable obligation to provide in-service opportunities which enable any teacher to overcome whatever deficiencies he may have — in understanding the learning process, for example, or perceiving the characteristics of his students, or following current developments in his field.

Community college teachers want well-designed and well-conducted in-service programs as one means of keeping professionally alive. However, they see the need for many other avenues of renewal. Striking in its common expression is the concern for staying abreast of developments in one's discipline and refreshing and upgrading oneself professionally. Few community colleges have sabbatical leave policies which can be judged adequate. Grants for summer study are few. Little federal or state money has been appropriated for such programs as the institutes funded by the National Science Foundation. Community college instructors strongly favor more opportunity for face-to-face work with their university colleagues. They report that heavy class loads often preclude their taking new approaches to teaching because no time is provided for planning. In many institutions funds are not available for faculties to participate in the sessions of professional associations in the various disciplines.

How to keep up, the greatest concern of the community college faculty member, is a major problem for administrators and policy makers from the community college district level up to the state capital and even beyond. A notable attack on this problem was signaled by action taken by the State of Florida in 1968. New legislation requires that three per cent of the amount designated for faculty salaries in the community colleges be utilized for faculty development. Apparently these funds can be used for leaves, in-service institutes and workshops, and similar activities. That other measures of this kind are needed urgently is beyond question:

> The accumulated testimony of faculty concerning their need for continuing study, increased associations with those in their own — and other — disciplines, and other means of professional improvement, indicates an apparent priority problem for junior colleges countrywide, not only now, but even more acutely in the immediate future. Though they generally agree philosophically and practically with the "open-door policy," many faculty have an almost foreboding sense that this policy and the national determination for education for "everyone who wants it after high school," may, unless large-scale provisions can be made for helping faculty, inexorably milk dry the major resource of their colleges: namely, the intellectual capital of its teachers.[7]

Faculty Participation in College Government

At least two other matters are high on the agenda of community college and faculty business. One has to do with the participation of faculty in the governance of the institution. At what points and by what means do they influence institutional policy and program development? In at least one state (California), legislative mandate requires the establishment of a faculty senate in each institution. Made up of faculty members, or their representatives, the senate advances their interests and provides a channel of communication with the administration. It deals with such things as educational policies, economic benefits, and personnel administration.

Of top priority in the community college, as in other educational institutions, is the need to clarify the respective areas of authority and responsibility of the board, the administration, the faculty, and the students. Although the community college is not alone in this need, it is at a stage of development where decisions pertaining to it are of extraordinary importance. They will determine whether the work of the college will be facilitated or molded to another set of purposes. Here the ancestral mix of secondary and higher education and the diversity of professional reference groups of the faculty make for perplexing problems. Which should serve as the model? The university? The public schools? Neither? A major reversal could result if there is uncritical transfer to community colleges of patterns of organization and procedures which have been forged by other institutions for their distinctive tasks. Few deny the need for change but the character of the change is all important. The machinery must be shaped to fit the mission.

Professional Affiliations of Faculty

Another question, related to the first, deals with the identity of the community college teacher. Where is his professional home? Beyond the campus where do his affiliations lie? Some say he belongs with organizations like the American Association of University Professors. Others suggest that membership in state or national affiliates of the National Education Association would be more suitable. In some cities community college faculty have joined with the American Federation of Teachers. And in a few cases the teachers have set up their own statewide association to speak for them at the state level. This problem takes on greater urgency and intensity because community college faculties are not only seeking identification with appropriate organizations beyond the campus but are also being sought by them — and in energetic fashion.

The issue of affiliation has not been decided. Nor is it likely that all faculty will identify with the same organizations. The diversified interests of community college teachers may prescribe affiliation with more than one group. But regardless of whether one organization is chosen or many, the critical issue is the possibility that organizations external to the community college will, as a result of value judgments required for membership, fragment this institution or divert it from its designated role.

Attracting a Talented Staff

The quality of faculty leadership is crucial to the success of the community college because the institutional aims and objectives have their ultimate translation in what is done in the classrooms, shops, and laboratories. What are the chances that community colleges can attract the kinds of people they really need? What will draw them? These institutions do not have the prestige of the Ivy League. The "professional stimulation" by graduate students is absent. How can the talent required for one of the most difficult and necessary jobs in American education be recruited?

A community college that exists by imitation will have no magnetism. An institution which can derive its own purposes only from the aims of other institutions will invite little interest. But hundreds of prospective community colleges, as well as existing ones, with greater reach, and a clear-cut assignment in American education, can win the personnel required. Talent finds its way to a promising, idealistic movement like the Peace Corps. It goes to Washington when creative ventures are anticipated. It now follows fresh political leadership to focus on the perplexities of the cities. This is the kind of talent that can be persuaded to help forge a new instrument to reach people who have not known such educational opportunity before and to help break the crust of educational custom. Whether the newness of these institutions will be noteworthy by chronology or creativity depends on the quality of staff leadership they can attract. Conversely, the quality of the staff will determine the character of the institutions. Nothing is more important, therefore, than the characteristics of the cadre which gives the college its initial impetus. Like an object moving in space, the community college will tend to persist in the direction first established. Ideally, the institution's leadership will be capable of the flexibility and responsiveness to permit rapid institutional adaptations, self-correction in programs, and a climate of experimentation.

NOTES

[1] San Mateo Junior College District, *District Policies and Procedures.* San Mateo, Calif., September 8, 1967.

[2] Research Division, National Education Association, *Teacher Supply and Demand in Universities, Colleges, and Junior Colleges, 1963–64 and 1964–65,* Research Report 1965-R4, Higher Education Series. Washington: National Education Association, April 1965.

[3] Bob Forbes, Dorothea Fry, and Jane Matson, *A Descriptive Study of New Full-Time Teachers in California Junior Colleges.* Modesto, Calif.: Executive Committee of the California Junior College Association, 1963.

[4] "A Consideration of Issues Affecting California Public Junior Colleges," staff report for presentation to the Coordinating Council for Higher Education, January 25–26, 1965, Sacramento, April 1965.

[5] Research Division, National Education Association, *op. cit.*

[6] Roger H. Garrison, *Junior College Faculty: Issues and Problems. A Preliminary National Appraisal.* Washington: American Association of Junior Colleges, 1967.

[7] *Ibid.*

7

FUTURE DEVELOPMENT: CONCERN AND CAUTION

The first problem of the junior college, then, is to establish itself in the educational firmament as a recognized step in the educational process. It must fight pressures to become what it is not. . . .

— Russell Lynes, "How Good Are the Junior Colleges?" *Harper's* (November 1966)

The community college was recently described as ". . . going down the educational superhighway hell for leather." That's the way it looked to Russell Lynes, then managing editor of *Harper's* magazine (November 1966). This impressive pace has won the attention of the nation's press both in the news columns and on the editorial pages. They have reported district organization, appointment of presidents, acquisition of sites, campus dedications, and zooming enrollments. In editorials and letters to the editor the community has stated hopes for what the institution would (or would not) do, and advocates of the college have made their claims of potential and performance.

That the community college is now a big segment of post-secondary education is a fact. That it is still in process of establishing its identity is apparent. That great expectations are held by its adherents is obvious. But the highway is not straight and clear enough to eliminate all uneasiness about the speed and direction or to remove the need for forethought so that risks can be minimized. Along with its promise, there are disquieting elements in the community college picture which must be faced.

Rapid Development

One of these is tied to the boom aspect of development. Institutions are founded almost overnight. Enrollments do not simply grow; they multiply. It is not unusual for a district to be established early in the calendar year, a president to be appointed in the spring, and the college to open in temporary quarters in the fall. In times of emergency, remarkable and unusual efforts are made. And the option of denying educational opportunity to several hundreds or even thousands of students by taking longer to get under way is not an attractive prospect. However, the community and all of those associated with the college need to know that sound establishment requires time and thoughtful consideration. A great many people ought to be involved in the process. Haste in the beginning will have its repercussions. The chances of success are improved if a minimum of a year's time is provided, and two years is better — with new facilities through standard construction allow three to four years.

Local Control

Another perplexing problem has its genesis in a kind of economic determinism. Frustrations and defeats brought about through inadequate local tax revenues have moved the community college in its search for funds to much larger district organization and driven it to state and federal sources of money. The resort to financial resources farther removed from the community has been accompanied by some loss of control. In a few states policy determination is largely at the state level, and the drift, if not purposive movement, is in that direction. What does this mean for community involvement and college responsiveness to community needs? The interfusing of community and college has been a distinctive and substantial justification for this kind of institution. Can it be maintained under direction from the state — or, for that matter, from districts almost as large as some states? How will things work in a metropolitan area where there is one board for a city of several million? If the institution is to continue to be community oriented and community serving, other organizational means are needed so that significant participation in the affairs of the college can be decentralized.

It has not been fully demonstrated that policy determination always has its locus where the money is. But it does seem clear that the community college of the future will be a different kind of institution if significant decisions about it are made without meaningful involvement of the people it serves. The necessary quest for sounder financial underpinnings will require accommodation to the value of localism with coaction of college and community. Each is important.

Diversification of Curriculums

No feature of the community college has more essential implications than its policy of open-door admissions. Without denying the social need, a question must be raised about the capacity of institutions to deliver on the implied promise. Here is one reason for concern in this regard: A much more diversified fare of educational programs is required than is commonly offered at present. In addition to transfer and occupational programs, general studies may be needed, with multiple program options for the students who neither transfer nor aim toward employment as highly skilled technicians. These students may lack academic ability or motivation (or both) for the increasingly difficult transfer and technical programs. Dorothy M. Knoell, in her studies of noncollege-bound youth in New York State, proposes that such a curriculum have a heavy core of social science content, including psychology and sociology, use communication skills laboratories to bring students up to a reasonable level of competence, offer opportunities for creative endeavors, and provide training and orientation for the countless beginning jobs which require little specialized knowledge and skill.[1] The curriculum would, in effect, be student oriented rather than university or career oriented, with the dual goal of assisting the student to discover what his potential is for education at higher levels in the established structure and preparing him to accept gainful employment in a career field.

Dr. Knoell also suggests the increasing need for planning varied programs of exploration, work experience, classroom study, field work, and out-of-class activities. She found that a large number of urban youth would not want to engage in full-time study after high school, even if it were offered without cost and in their home communities. Although most acknowledged the need for further education to help them on the job, at the same time they wanted the security of regular employment after high school and the feeling of success which was so often lacking in their high school experience. From the standpoint of learning, work-study programs of part-time day enrollment in only two or three courses seem more likely to produce good results among the less able urban youth than full-time day programs of fifteen units or more or part-time evening programs after a whole day on the job. Successful job experience helps build a more satisfactory self-image, which in turn increases the probability of successful classroom experience.

Remedial programs, a full range of student personnel services, and plenty of faculty time are other necessary ingredients if the educational needs of all who come because of the open-door policy are to be met. An educational approach of these dimensions should not be sold to the public on the basis of low cost. Generous financial support is essential. However, it can be justified as a financial investment which will pay off in terms of both individual and community betterment. The point is, no one must be fooled into believing that the open door means the usual college curriculums at community college bargain prices. Nor should anyone delude himself that opportunity consists in simply allowing the student to enter; it involves matching the student with a suitable pattern of learning. If that pattern does not exist, then opportunity does not exist, even if the student is on the registrar's official list.

Each institution needs to determine how comprehensive it can be and how open in admissions policy. However, a word of caution is in order: a latent tendency to limit access must not be rationalized in the name of prudence. Educational needs will be met — if not by community colleges then by other kinds of educational institutions. And, to be sure, in time such institutions might be required. But let this be a rational decision by society upon the basis of perceived need, not a result of rigidity in the community college or its failure to convince the community that the proposed breadth of services merits support.

Tuition Policies

How much of the financial load should be carried by the student? This is another pressing issue. As already pointed out, community colleges usually charge little or no tuition. But mounting costs of many public services, including education, have brought intensive investigation of all possible sources of revenue, and recurrently the student is looked to for a larger contribution. In addition to the obvious reason that larger payments by the student will make more money available to the colleges, justifications for tuition charges are adduced. For example, those who most directly benefit from education should shoulder the cost. (This suggests that the individual receives the greater or even sole benefit.) If the student does not pay something, he will not appreciate his opportunity; his degree of effort will be proportionate to the money he puts up. Reasons such as these last ones are largely matters of conjecture. With regard to benefits, it can be held that a highly complex society requires an enlightened citizenry if sound public policy is to be formulated and a democratic order is to be maintained. And unless there are people competent in medicine, law, technologies, economic activities, and public service, our cultural aspirations and expectations stand little chance of achievement. With its many programs, including community services and continuing education, the community college can marshal substantial evidence that since the community as a whole benefits through educational opportunity the most equitable way to finance the services is by public funds.

The President of the Milwaukee Vocational, Technical and Adult Schools has estimated that one class, completing its work in June 1967, increased the economic wealth of the community by the amount of $186,570,000 payable over the next 30 years. He calculated that the more than 2000 students who had taken one or two-year programs leading to an industrial or business competence had increased their earning power as a result of those educational programs by $1.50 per hour as a conservative estimate. In restricting his observations to the measurable increased earning power of individuals he arrived at a dollar amount which supported his assertion that the school of vocational, technical, and adult education is the greatest natural resource possessed by the City of Milwaukee; and that the vocational, technical, and adult educational system is the greatest natural resource of the entire state of Wisconsin. Whether or not the other educational institutions of that state concur in his views, it is true that economists have come up with persuasive evidence that education is not only a good investment for individuals, but is an important key to the nation's economic growth. They regard investment in education as capital embodied in people — "human capital" — that is as important as the "nonhuman capital" embodied in plant and equipment.

Increased earning power thus means increased savings as well as more money for homes, food, clothing, amusements, education, utilities, and taxes. Taxation is thus, in a very real sense, deferred payment of tuition.

Many of the current arguments in favor of higher charges to the student are remarkably like those used two generations ago to oppose public high schools. The requirements of life are now such that two more years of education are commonly needed and therefore are justified as a public expense. The National Commission on Technology, Automation, and Economic Progress is the most recent in a long line of national commissions to urge that "A nationwide system of free public education through two years beyond high school should be established."[2]

In some states there are practical difficulties in the immediate removal of student charges. But the elimination of these charges should become policy if the community college is to forward the goal of universal educational opportunity and be a means of economic and social mobility. Once the principle of tuition is established, no matter how small the amount at the outset, almost inexorable pressures will result in gradual but continuous increase. It may be that the degree of opportunity is reduced in proportion to the increase in fees. Therefore, to push this reasoning to its logical conclusion, a truly open-door institution will make no financial demand on the student.

Administrative Policies

Another hazard for the fast-moving community college is fragmentation of the institution and a skewing of its purposes unless an organization can be designed to accomplish its objectives. In most colleges and universities concepts of educational administration and governance are under test and in process of change. Strains are potentially more acute in the community college for several reasons: the heterogeneity of students and faculty; explosive growth and proliferation of new institutions — colleges without traditions and established leadership structures; and the evolution of role definitions for faculty, students, and administration in an institution still determining its logical forms of organization — forms that have their basis in perceptions of the job to be done. But this is more than a matter of organization. It is also a problem of leadership. Without doubt, among many issues and concerns, one of the most serious is the need for an alert and highly competent leadership throughout the institution so that a productive equilibrium can be maintained.

Careful and orderly development of the institution, effective communication with the community, determination of suitable educational programs, securing of financial means, and accommodation of the forces within the institution toward constructive ends are all possible through able leadership. But the supply falls far short of the demand. A number of universities have looked for faculty members of senior grade to head up programs to prepare community college teachers and administrators. These "teachers of teachers" are critically needed. Most of the states either already have or are establishing state-level offices with responsibility for community college development. In either case, they are seeking qualified staff. Personnel with community college expertise also are sought by the U.S. Office of Education and by the foundations.

Moreover, the current annual requirement for new community college presidents is well over a hundred, and large institutions each require a number of broadly prepared administrative officers in instruction, finance, student personnel, community relations, institutional research, and governmental relations. One of the key leadership responsibilities in the institution is held by the chairman of the department or division, and here the shortage is crucial. For many of the top-level posts a game of musical chairs is in progress. The same names have a way of appearing on the lists of candidates for positions all the way from local institutions to the national scene.

Some feel that the apparent short supply of experienced and able people is not all bad because it has had the effect of sharply increasing the level of salaries and perquisites, but developments in the community colleges urgently require that potential talent in these institutions be identified and cultivated and that large numbers of capable people be recruited. If it were just a matter of filling the positions that exist in newly established and expanding institutions, the problem would be serious enough, but in many ways the course is still being charted and leadership in such an enterprise calls for special qualities.

Although the efforts to date, including the Junior College Leadership Program, have helped, they are not enough to show a net gain in solving the problem. There should be no doubt in anybody's mind that the developmental activities now necessary go far beyond the scale of previous attempts. Not only is participation by both governmental and private interests called for, but every responsible person in each institution is under obligation to look for and to nurture talent. The whole field will be served.

Leadership and Future Direction

Community college leadership should reach beyond its own institutions. As part of the worldwide educational community, its spokesmen must be articulate about their experience and report it to colleagues with different missions in education. One possible outcome would be adaptation of the community college idea to unmet educational needs in other cultures.

In the early days of the junior college, the leading theorists were university presidents — among them Harper of the University of Chicago, Tappan of the University of Michigan, and Folwell of the University of Minnesota. Later came Conant of Harvard University and Professors Koos of the University of Chicago and Eels of Stanford. Now there is unquestioned need for those who know the community college well through their own administrative practice and teaching experience to step up communication with both national and international educational leadership. And this assertion leads to a final expression of concern: the institution's concept of itself.

No more important factor than this exists in determining the direction and significance of community college development. Nothing will further its work more than its recognition and acceptance of its own individuality in a context of relationships. The community college is necessary. It has emerged out of societal needs and aspirations. These are the sources of its identity. Its greatest worth will be achieved as it confidently takes hold of its special assignment as an institution in its own right within a complete program of educational services throughout the nation. The community college is a member of the educational family — a member that needs to share in family conversation and to carry its part of the total family responsibility. Not only will it benefit from this association but it has something unique and vital to give.

NOTES

[1] Dorothy M. Knoell, *Toward Educational Opportunity for All.* Albany: State University of New York, 1966.

[2] National Commission on Technology, Automation, and Economic Progress. *Op. cit., Technology and the American Economy.* Washington: U.S. Government Printing Office, 1966.

BIBLIOGRAPHY

More detailed information may be of interest to the large numbers of people now taking on various responsibilities in community colleges. The list of references that follows is not intended to cover all aspects of the field but only those that are especially relevant to the establishment of new institutions and to the clarifying of the community college's role in relation to the roles of other educational organizations.

Legislation

The Commission on Legislation of the American Association of Junior Colleges prepared a statement of principles to be incorporated in state legislative action bearing on community colleges. Later, with the principles as a base, representatives of the Association cooperated with the Council of State Governments in drafting a model bill for the guidance of state legislators.

American Association of Junior Colleges. *Principles of Legislative Action for Community Junior Colleges.* Washington: The Association, 1962. 18 pp. 40 cents.

Community Junior College Act. (Available from the Council of State Governments, 1313 East Sixtieth Street, Chicago, Illinois, 60637. January 1965. 10 pp. Free.

Faculty

A competent observer and reporter was asked to spend a year visiting community college campuses and listening to faculty members describe their feelings about their work. The aim was to get at the problems confronting the teachers in community colleges as they saw them, so that both pre-service and in-service activities designed to raise the level of competence would be realistic and effective. The study was funded by the United States Steel Foundation.

Garrison, Roger H. *Junior College Faculty: Issues and Problems*. Washington: American Association of Junior Colleges, 1967. 90 pp. $2.00.

Garrison, Roger H. *Teaching in a Junior College*. Washington: American Association of Junior Colleges and American Education Publishers Institute, 1968. 28 pp. $1.50.

Student Personnel

A two-year intensive examination of student personnel services was conducted under the leadership of a national committee headed by T. R. McConnell, then chairman of the Center for the Study of Higher Education at the University of California at Berkeley. Project director was Max R. Raines of Michigan State University. The study involved visits by experienced investigators to a large proportion of the nation's community colleges. Out of these efforts came a report to the Carnegie Corporation, which funded the project. This detailed publication, entitled *Junior College Student Personnel Programs — Appraisal and Development,* was condensed in nontechnical language by Charles C. Collins, a member of the advisory committee.

Collins, Charles C. *Junior College Student Personnel Programs: What They Are and What They Should Be*. Washington: American Association of Junior Colleges, 1967. 46 pp. $1.50.

Establishment

How does a community college go about organizing itself after the president is selected? Professor B. Lamar Johnson of the University of California at Los Angeles visited more than forty new institutions to ascertain what was done and the sequence of steps. An advisory committee of experienced community college administrators assisted him in preparation of a guide to the establishment of new institutions.

Johnson, B. Lamar. *Starting a Community Junior College.* Washington: American Association of Junior Colleges, 1964. 91 pp. $1.00.

Occupational Education

Occupational education, or vocational-technical education at the postsecondary school level, has had a hard fight in winning the attention of institutions of higher education. One of the first and most significant signs of a change in attitude was action by the American Council on Education in 1963, through its Commission on Academic Affairs, to assess the place of occupational education within education and within a new technological economy. Grant Venn was appointed to direct the study and write the report, which includes important references to the place of occupational education in the community college.

One of the most useful and popular interpretations of technical education in the junior college was prepared by Norman Harris of the University of Michigan, a former director of technical education in a California junior college. The publication was a project of the Curriculum Commission of the American Association of Junior Colleges and was supported in part by the Alfred P. Sloan Foundation.

With the assistance of the same foundation, the Association surveyed activities in the health fields to identify programs that could serve as prototypes for new colleges and for institutions embarking on new courses of study. Robert E. Kinsinger, a nationally recognized authority in education for health careers, conducted the investigation.

A number of other reports are coming out of an Association project financed by the W. K. Kellogg Foundation. A series of publications in the occupational fields of health, business, industry-science, and public service is in preparation. One report, on hospitality education, has been completed.

Another important publication is the result of collaboration of the National Health Council and the American Association of Junior Colleges under financial assistance by the U.S. Office of Education. The *Guide for Health Technology Program Planning* is among the finest examples of cooperation between educational institutions and professional associations in curriculum development.

Almarode, Richard L. *Guidelines for Hospitality Education in Junior Colleges.* Washington: American Association of Junior Colleges, 1967. 56 pp. $1.50.

AAJC-NHC Committee on Health Technology Education. *A Guide for Health Technology Program Planning.* Washington: American Association of Junior Colleges and National Health Council, 1967. 52 pp. $1.00.

Crockett, Thomas S., and Stinchcomb, James D. *Guidelines for Law Enforcement Programs in Community Junior Colleges.* Washington: American Association of Junior Colleges, 1968. 32 pp. $1.50.

Harris, Norman C. *Technical Education in the Junior College: New Programs for New Jobs.* Washington: American Association of Junior Colleges, 1964. 102 pp. $1.25.

Kinsinger, Robert E. *Education for Health Technicians: An Overview.* Washington: American Association of Junior Colleges, 1965. 35 pp. $1.00.

Riendeau, Albert J. *The Role of the Advisory Committee in Occupational Education in the Junior College.* Washington: American Association of Junior Colleges, 1967. 75 pp. $1.50.

Venn, Grant. *Man, Education, and Work.* Washington: American Council on Education, 1964. 184 pp. $1.50.

Facilities

The Educational Facilities Laboratories, Inc., 447 Madison Avenue, New York, New York, has a large number of publications of interest to those planning academic facilities. It also currently supports a facilities information service through the American Association of Junior Colleges. An arrangement has been made for a series of architects to spend a year on a leave of absence from their firms to head up this clearinghouse service. Conferences are conducted on facilities problems in the community college field, kits of information are sent to new institutions, lists are kept of sources of materials, and publications are put out. A number of articles have appeared in the Junior College Journal which take up various aspects of facilities planning. Two conference reports are now available and others are being prepared. One of the former deals with facilities for the inner-city community college and the other with plans for student personnel facilities.

Collins, Charles C. *Premises: Planning Student Personnel Facilities.* Washington: American Association of Junior Colleges, 1967. 26 pp. $1.00.

Primer for Planners. Washington: American Association of Junior Colleges, 1967. 48 pages, $1.50.

Reed, Bob H. and Harper, William A. *The College Facilities Thing: Impressions of an Airborne Seminar.* Washington: American Association of Junior Colleges, 1968. 72 pages, $2.50.

Richardson, Richard C., Jr. *The Interim Campus: Starting New Community Junior Colleges.* Washington: American Association of Junior Colleges, 1968. 38 pages, $1.50.

Weidenthal, Bud. *The Community College Commitment to the Inner City.* Washington: American Association of Junior Colleges, 1967. 12 pp. 75 cents.

Transfer to Four-year Colleges

What problems do community college students have in moving to four-year institutions? How can two-year and four-year colleges work together more closely to the advantage of the transferring student? To find out, a national committee requested the Center for the Study of Higher Education at the University of California to follow up a national sample of junior college students to see what happened. A grant from the U.S. Office of Education supported the research. Based upon the study report which was prepared by Dorothy M. Knoell and Leland L. Medsker of the University, a number of guidelines were formulated to facilitate transfer. Those were refined in a series of state conferences in which representatives of both junior and senior colleges participated. James H. Nelson directed this year-long activity under a grant from the Esso Foundation. At the request of the committee the results of the research study, as well as the guidelines statement, were published by the American Council on Education. Three of its member organizations comprised the steering committee: the Association of American Colleges, the American Association of Junior Colleges, and the American Association of Collegiate Registrars and Admissions Officers.

> *Guidelines for Improving Articulation Between Junior and Senior Colleges.* A statement by the Joint Committee of AAC, AAJC, AACRAO. Washington: American Council on Education, 1966.

> Knoell, Dorothy M., and Medsker, Leland L. *From Junior to Senior College: A National Study of the Transfer Student.* Washington: American Council on Education, 1965. 102 pp. $2.50.

Research

As indicated previously, a great deal of research is now being conducted in the community college field. A systematic and up-to-date inventory of this activity is kept by the Educational Resources Information Center at the University of California at Los Angeles. This center, designated as the Clearing House for Junior College Information, works closely with the American Association of Junior Colleges and is funded by the U.S. Office of Education. The Clearing House acquires, indexes, abstracts, and disseminates research documents and research-related materials in the junior college field. Recently the American Association of Junior Colleges requested an updating of a bibliography of doctoral dissertations on the junior college. The following publications are examples of the service now available through the Center.

> ERIC Clearing House for Junior College Information. *The Junior and Community College — A Bibliography of Doctoral Dissertations 1964–1966.* Washington: American Association of Junior Colleges, 1967. 17 pp. $1.00.

Rouche, John E. *Salvage, Redirection, or Custody?* Washington: American Association of Junior Colleges, 1968. 67 pages, $2.00.

Works of General Interest and Textbooks

Those who want to know more about the early days of the community and junior colleges can refer to the voluminous work of Leonard V. Koos published by the University of Minnesota in 1924. Koos dedicated his study to William Watts Folwell, president emeritus of the University of Minnesota, who, in Koos's estimation, "more than a half century ago foreshadowed the junior college movement." Another monumental treatment is that by Walter Crosby Eels, then a professor at Stanford University and editor of the *Junior College Journal.* Eels argued for a 6–3–3–2 form of educational organization as contrasted with the 6–4–4 plan, which appealed to Koos. Although the Eels plan is the dominant one now, there are substantial reasons for continuing consideration of principles embodied in organization of a unit that brackets the present last two years of high school and first two years of college work.

Jesse P. Bogue was the first author to develop a book on the community college concept. Interestingly, he had been president of a private residential junior college in Vermont — Green Mountain Junior College — and had left there to become executive secretary of the American Association of Junior Colleges. His deep and growing interest in the public community college led to the publication of his book in 1950.

In 1956 further attention was directed to the public junior college as a result of the decision of the National Society for the Study of Education in Chicago to publish a yearbook on the junior college. Adult education programs and community services were given new and important emphasis. Then in 1960, as part of a series of investigations conducted by the Center for the Study of Higher Education at Berkeley under the broad title "The Diversification of American Higher Education," Leland Medsker published *The Junior College: Progress and Prospect.*

Dr. Medsker knew junior colleges well through firsthand administrative experience and intensive research. His was the most evaluative of the reports up to the time of his writing. The Carnegie Corporation provided partial support for the study. At the present time Medsker is preparing another research-based report which will bring up to date his important but now slightly aged findings.

Another significant book appeared in 1960 as part of the Carnegie Series in American Education: Burton Clark's *The Open Door College — A Case Study.* Clark is a sociologist who was then with the Berkeley Center. His examination of a public junior college (city college) in San Jose gives some valuable insights into the characteristics of community college students and the process of reconciling aspirations with realistic educational goals.

James W. Thornton's book, published in 1960 and revised in 1967, is a useful manual of operations. Thornton, a professor at California State College at San Jose, is a former community college dean.

Still another valuable sociological approach to junior colleges is that by Blocker, Plummer, and Richardson. It is of particular worth with respect to the implications of a diversified student body for the organization of the college and curriculum development.

Blocker, Clyde E.; Plummer, Robert H.; and Richardson, Richard C., Jr. *The Two-Year College: A Social Synthesis.* Englewood Cliffs, N.J.: Prentice-Hall, 1965. 298 pp. $8.25.

Bogue, Jesse Parker. *The Community College.* New York: McGraw-Hill Book Co., 1950. 390 pp.

Clark, Burton R. *The Open-Door College: A Case Study.* New York: McGraw-Hill Book Co., 1960. 207 pp. $5.95.

Eels, Walter Crosby. *The Junior College.* Cambridge, Mass.: The Riverside Press, 1931. 833 pp.

Fields, Ralph R. *The Community College Movement.* New York: McGraw-Hill Book Co., 1962.

Henry, Nelson B. (ed.). *The Public Junior College.* Chicago: University of Chicago Press, 1956. 347 pp.

Koos, Leonard Vincent. *The Junior College.* Minneapolis: University of Minnesota, 1924. 682 pp. $5.00.

Medsker, Leland L. *The Junior College: Progress and Prospect.* New York: McGraw-Hill Book Co., 1960. 367 pp. $6.95.

Thornton, James W., Jr. *The Community Junior College.* New York: John Wiley & Sons, 1960. 300 pp. $7.25.

National Developments

One of the fascinating things about the community college is its emergence in an environment of tradition and attitude which varies from state to state or region to region. An account of this process is given in abbreviated and informal style for twenty of the states in a book called, simply, *Junior Colleges: 20 States.*

For detailed information about more than 750 junior colleges in the United States, the Canal Zone, and Puerto Rico, a standard reference is *American Junior Colleges,* published every four years by the American Council on Education. This is particularly helpful to guidance counselors and prospective students.

Continuing information about junior colleges throughout the country is given in the *Junior College Journal,* published by the American Association of Junior Colleges. It is widely read not only by faculty and administrative personnel but by board members and university representatives. The Association also publishes an annual directory of junior colleges, both private and public, as well as other bulletins in such fields as occupational education, student personnel services, and legislation.

American Association of Junior Colleges. *1968 Junior College Directory.* Washington: The Association, 1968. 97 pp. $1.50.

American Association of Junior Colleges. *Junior Colleges: 20 States.* Washington: The Association, 1966. 178 pp. $2.00.

Federal Affairs Bulletin. Washington: American Association of Junior Colleges. Occasional reports. Free.

Gleazer, Edmund J., Jr. (ed.). *American Junior Colleges.* Washington: American Council on Education, 1967. 957 pp. $14.00.

Junior College Journal. Washington: American Association of Junior Colleges. $4.00 per year. 75 cents per single copy.

Occupational Education Bulletin. Washington: American Association of Junior Colleges. Occasional reports. Free.

INDEX

147